Arthur Latham Perry

Scotch-Irish in New England

Arthur Latham Perry

Scotch-Irish in New England

ISBN/EAN: 9783743329584

Manufactured in Europe, USA, Canada, Australia, Japa

Cover: Foto ©ninafisch / pixelio.de

Manufactured and distributed by brebook publishing software
(www.brebook.com)

Arthur Latham Perry

Scotch-Irish in New England

SCOTCH-IRISH IN NEW ENGLAND.

BY

REV. A. L. PERRY, D.D., LL.D.,

PROFESSOR OF HISTORY AND POLITICAL ECONOMY IN WILLIAMS COLLEGE,
WILLIAMSTOWN, MASS.

BOSTON:
PRINTED BY J. S. CUSHING & CO.
1891.

Typography by J. S. Cushing & Co., Boston.

Presswork by Berwick & Smith, Boston.

READ BEFORE THE SCOTCH-IRISH SOCIETY OF AMERICA, AT PITTSBURGH, PENN., MAY 29, 1890; AND HERE REPRINTED WITH THEIR CONSENT.

SCOTCH–IRISH IN NEW ENGLAND.

———∘∘⦂⊛⦂∘∘———

Mr. President and Brethren of the Society—

The Scotch-Irish did not enter New England unheralded. Early in the spring of 1718 Rev. Mr. Boyd was dispatched from Ulster to Boston as an agent of some hundreds of those people who expressed a strong desire to remove to New England, should suitable encouragement be afforded them. His mission was to Governor Shute, of Massachusetts, then in the third year of his administration of that colony, an old soldier of King William, a Lieutenant-Colonel under Marlborough in the wars of Queen Anne, and wounded in one of the great battles in Flanders. Mr. Boyd was empowered to make all necessary arrangements with the civil authorities for the reception of those whom he represented, in case his report of the state of things here should prove to be favorable.

As an assurance to the governor of the good faith and earnest resolve of those who sent him, Mr. Boyd brought an engrossed parchment twenty-eight inches square, containing the following memorial to his excellency, and the autograph names of the heads of the families proposing to emigrate: "We whose names are underwritten, Inhabitants of ye North of Ireland, Doe in our own names, and in the names of many others, our Neighbors, Gentlemen, Ministers, Farmers, and Tradesmen, Commissionate and appoint our trusty and well beloved friend, the Reverend Mr. William Boyd, of Macasky, to His Excellency, the Right Honorable Collonel Samuel Suitte, Governour of New England, and to assure His Excellency of our sincere and hearty Inclination to Transport ourselves to that very excellent and renowned Plantation upon our obtaining from His Excellency suitable incouragement. And further to act and Doe in our Names as his prudence shall direct. Given under our hands this 26th day of March, Anno Dom. 1718."

To this brief but explicit memorial, three hundred and nineteen names were appended, all but thirteen of them in fair and vigorous

5

autograph. Thirteen only, or four per cent of the whole, made their "mark" upon the parchment. It may well be questioned, whether in any other part of the United Kingdom at that time, one hundred and seventy-two years ago, in England or Wales, or Scotland or Ireland, so large a proportion as ninety-six per cent of promiscuous householders in the common walks of life could have written their own names. And it was proven in the sequel, that those who could write, as well as those who could not, were also able upon occasion to make their "*mark.*"

I have lately scrutinized with critical care this ancient parchment stamped by the hands of our ancestors, now in the custody of the Historical Society of New Hampshire, and was led into a line of reflections which I will not now repeat, as to its own vicissitudes in the seven quarter-centuries of its existence, and as to the personal vicissitudes and motives, and heart-swellings and hazards, and cold and hunger and nakedness, as well as the hard-earned success and the sense of triumph, and the immortal *vestigia* of the men who lovingly rolled and unrolled this costly parchment on the banks of the Foyle and the Bann Water! Tattered are its edges now, shrunken by time and exposure its original dimensions, illegible already some of the names even under the fortifying power of modern lenses, but precious in the eyes of New England, nay, precious in the eyes of Scotch-Irishmen everywhere, is this venerable muniment of intelligence and of courageous purpose looking down upon us from the time of the first English George.

It is enough for our present purpose to know that Governor Shute gave such general encouragement and promise of welcome through Mr. Boyd to his constituents that the latter were content with the return-word received from their messenger, and set about with alacrity the preparations for their embarkation. Nothing definite was settled between the governor and the minister, not even the locality of a future residence for the newcomers; but it is clear in general, that the governor's eye was upon the district of Maine, then and for a century afterward, a part of Massachusetts. Five years before Boyd's visit to Boston, had been concluded the European treaty of Utrecht, and, as between England and France, it had therein been agreed that all of Nova Scotia or Acadia, "according to its ancient boundaries," should remain to England. But what were the ancient boundaries of Acadia? Did it include all that is now New Brunswick? Or had France still a large territory on the Atlantic between Acadia and Maine? This was a vital question, wholly unsolved by the treaty. The motive of Massachusetts in welcoming the Scotch-Irish into her jurisdiction was to plant them on the frontiers of Maine as a living bulwark against the restless and enterprising French of the north, and their still more restless savage allies; the motive of the Ulstermen in coming to America was to establish homes of their own in fee simple, taxable only to support their own form of worship and their strictly local needs — to escape, in short, the *land lease* and the *church tithe;* the bottom aims, accordingly, of both parties to the negotiation ran parallel with each other, and there was in consequence a swift agreement in the present, and in the long sequel a large realization of the purposes of both.

August 4, 1718, five small ships came to anchor near the little wharf at the foot of State Street in Boston, then a town of perhaps twelve thousand people. On board these ships were about one hundred and twenty families of Scotch-Irish. They reckoned themselves in families. It is certain that the number of persons in the average family so reckoned was, according to our modern notions, very large. There may have been, there probably was, at least seven hundred and fifty passengers on board. Cluttered in those separate ships, not knowing exactly whither to turn, having as a whole no recognized leader on board, no Castle Garden to afford a preliminary shelter, no organized Commissioners of Immigration to lend them a hand, the most of them extremely poor — the imagination would fain, but may not picture the confusions and perplexities, the stout hearts of some and the heart-aches of others, the reckless joy of children, and the tottering steps of old men and women. One patriarch, John Young — I know his posterity well — was ninety-five years old. And there were babies in arms, a plenty of them!

Besides Mr. Boyd, who had stayed the summer in Boston, where he found already settled a few scattered and peeled of his own race and faith, there were three Presbyterian ministers on board, — Mr. McGregor, of blessed memory, Mr. Cornwell, and Mr. Holmes. Those best off of all the passengers — the McKeens, the Cargills, the Nesmiths, the Cochrans, the Dinsmores, the Mooars, and some other families — were natives of Scotland, whose heads had passed over into Ulster during the short reign of James II. These were Covenanters. They had lived together in the valley of the Bann Water for about thirty years, in or near the towns of Coleraine and Ballymoney and Kilrea. Their pastor was James McGregor. They wished to settle together in the new land of promise. They or their fathers and neighbors had felt the edge of the sword of Graham of Claverhouse in Argyleshire; they wished to enjoy together in peace in some sequestered spot the sweet ministrations of the Gospel according to their own sense of its rule and order, and, being better able than the rest to wait and choose out for themselves, we shall follow their fortunes a little farther on.

Others of the company were the descendants of those who participated in the original "Colonization of Ulster," which dates from 1610; and of those who, three years later, formed the first Presbytery in Ireland, the "Presbytery of Antrim." Others still were the progeny of those Scotchmen and Englishmen, whom Cromwell transplanted at the middle of the century to take the places of those wasted by his own pitiless sword — "the sword of the Lord and of Gideon!" And a few families of native Irish also mingled in the throngs around the wharf, doubtless drawn by sympathy and attachment to take the risk of the New with their neighbors whom they had found trustworthy and hospitable in the Old. I only know for certain that the numerous Young family, consisting of four generations, and the wife of Joshua Gray, of whom we shall hear more pretty soon, were Celtic Irish.

If now we except some individuals and families of this great company, who found pretty soon a transient or permanent home in Boston in connection with their countrymen already settled there in an isolated way, and who a few years afterward formed a Presbyterian Church in Long Lane (later Federal Street), under Rev. John Moorehead of saintly but eccentric memory, which church turned Congregational in 1786, and afterward, under the famous Dr. Channing, became the bridge to Unitarianism; and if we except also, perhaps, as many families who went up that autumn to Andover, then a new town whose development they influenced both socially and theologically, and a considerable number more who went up temporarily to await events, to the towns along the Merrimac, as Dracut and Haverhill, all the rest of the migration became located in the course of six months in three main centers, to which we must now attend in order, and from which these peculiar people diffused themselves little by little into every corner of New England.

1. WORCESTER. Nowadays we in Massachusetts call Worcester "the heart of the Commonwealth." It is a shallow bowl of beautiful country. The fall of 1718 marked the fifth year of its permanent settlement. There were about fifty log-houses and two hundred souls within the circle. These were all English and Puritans, and from the towns immediately to the eastward. But the Indians were hostile. Two previous settlements on the spot had been abandoned from this cause, — the first in King Philip's War in the

year 1675, the second in Queen Anne's War in 1709. Now the colony was determined to hold the ground. At least five garrison-houses, one a regular block fort, stood within the bowl. Accordingly, Governor Shute looked favorably upon the proposition, that a part of the Scotch-Irish, now in one sense on his hands, should go direct to Worcester, to find a much-needed home for themselves, to reinforce the fifty families already on the ground, and to take their chances in helping to defend the menaced western frontier, fifty miles from Boston.

We do not know exactly how many went to Worcester. We may fairly infer that at least fifty families — large families — went straight from Boston to Worcester that autumn, and that the population of the place was thus more than doubled at one stroke. I entertain the opinion, gathered from scattered and uncertain data, that it was the poorer, the more illiterate, the more helpless, part of the five ship-loads who were conducted to Worcester. I have hanging in my study, handsomely framed, the original deed by which my immediate maternal ancestor, Matthew Gray, conveyed to his son, of the same name, in 1735, his farm in Worcester of fifty-five acres, still called there the "Gray Farm," to which deed are appended not the autographs but the "marks" of Matthew and Jean, his wife. Neither Matthew nor Jean could write. The deed is witnessed, however, by "William Gray, Jr.," who writes a fair hand; but "Ealanor Gray," who witnesses with him, makes her "mark." Three marks to one manual is a bad proportion, but you will allow me to premise that the Grays, though illiterate, were long-headed.

There is much evidence that the poor Scotch-Irish were welcomed in Worcester at first. They were needed there, both for civil and military reasons. Jonas Rice, the first permanent settler of Worcester, who had been a planter during the second settlement broken up by the Indians, returned to his farm to stay, October 21, 1713, and remained with his family alone in the forest till the spring of 1715. Adonijah, his son, was the first child born in Worcester, November 7, 1714. The cool courage, good sense, and strict integrity of Jonas Rice made him the first great leader in the town where great leaders have never been wanting since. He was just the man to appreciate the stout hearts of his new-come, not yet well-understood, neighbors. No town organization had as yet been made when, in 1722, Lovell's Indian War broke out, and two Scotch-Irishmen, John Gray and Robert Crawford, were posted alone as scouts on Leicester Hill to the westward, doubtless at Rice's in-

stance. In September of the same year a township organization
was first effected, and John Gray, with Jonas Rice, were two of the
first selectmen; William Gray was chosen one of the two fence-
viewers, and Robert Peebles one of the two hog-reeves. At the first
annual town meeting, the next year, new names of the strangers
appear on the list of town officers; for example, James Hamilton as surveyor, and Andrew Farren as fence-viewer, though John
Gray dropped this year from selectman to sealer of leather; but at
the second annual March meeting, 1724, John Gray goes back to
his earlier post as selectman; James McClellan, great-great-great-
grandfather to the late general-in-chief, becomes a constable; Robert
Lethridge, a surveyor of highways; William Gray and Robert Peebles, fence-viewers; John Battay, tithingman; and Matthew Gray,
my own great-great-grandfather, both sealer of leather and hog-reeve.

The most interesting of the purely Irish families, who came with
the Scotch to Worcester, with whom they had contracted relation-
ship during their long residence in Ulster, or become attached by
community of sentiment and suffering, was the Young family, four
generations together. They brought the potato to Worcester, and
it was first planted there in several fields in the spring of 1719.
The tradition is still lively in Scotch-Irish families (I listened to it
eagerly in my boyhood) that some of their English neighbors, after
enjoying the hospitality of one of the Irish families, were presented
each, on their departure, with a few tubers for planting, and the
recipients, unwilling to give offense by refusing, accepted the gift;
but suspecting the poisonous quality, carried them only to the next
swamp and *chucked* them into the water. The same spring a few
potatoes were given for seed to a Mr. Walker, of Andover, Mass.,
by an Irish family who had wintered with him, previous to their
departure for Londonderry to the northward. The potatoes were
accordingly planted, came up and flourished well, blossomed and
produced *balls*, which the family supposed were the fruit to be eaten.
They cooked the balls in various ways, but could not make them
palatable, and pronounced them unfit for food. The next spring,
while plowing the garden, the plow passed through where the
potatoes had grown, and turned out some of great size, by which
means they discovered their mistake. This is the reason why this
now indispensable esculent is still called in New England certainly,
and perhaps elsewhere, the "Irish potato."

John Young was perhaps the oldest immigrant who ever came to
this country to live and die. If the inscription on his tombstone is
to be trusted, which the American Antiquarian Society, of Worcester,

copied and published many years ago, he was ninety-five years old
when he landed at Boston. He lived in Worcester twelve years,
died in 1730, was buried in the old yard on the common. His son,
David Young, an old man when he came, died at ninety-four years,
and was buried in the same place. *His* son, William Young, a
stone-cutter by trade, erected over their graves a common double
headstone, with the following inscriptions in parallel columns, united
at the bottom by the rude yet precious rhyming lines: —

"Here lies interred the remains of
John Young, who was born in
the isle of Bert, near Londonderry, in the Kingdom of Ireland.
He departed this life, June
30, 1730, aged 107 years.

Here lies interred the remains of
David Young, who was born in
the parish of Tahbeyn, county of
Donegal, and Kingdom of Ireland.
He departed this life, December
26, aged 94 years.

The aged son, and the more aged father
Beneath (these) stones their mould'ring bones
Here rest together."

Moses Young, probably the son of this epitaphist, William Young,
was a lad of some six years at the time of the emigration, and
became the ancestor of numerous families of that name in Western
Massachusetts, and particularly in Williamstown, the town of my
residence, where there are no less than five Young families at
present, living in one neighborhood, the same they have occupied as
farmers for a century and a quarter. These families and individuals
have never exhibited the main traits of their Scotch-Irish companions and their descendants. They have been less "canny" and
enterprising. Race blood tells from generation to generation. They
have been, perhaps, more inclined to intoxicants than the others;
although, if the truth must be told, the whole tribe in New England,
as a rule, and in the earlier times, *have drunk more than their fair
share of the liquor.* Only now and then one of the Youngs has tried
professional and official life. John Young, born in Worcester, June
2, 1739, studied medicine with the first and famous Dr. Green, of
Worcester. He practiced a little while in Pelham, and then moved
to Peterborough, N.H., about 1764. Both of these were Scotch-
Irish towns, and Dr. Young's migrations illustrate the usage, well-
nigh universal in the last century, of families and individuals
moving from town to town within the Presbyterian circuit. Young
was always very poor, and became very intemperate. The common
custom of "treating" the doctor and minister at each professional,
and even friendly call, wrought mischief to multitudes of both
orders; and the later and the last necessities of poor John Young,

who died February 27, 1807, were considerately ministered unto by the town of Peterborough.

When "Lovell's War" was over, and before the "Old French War" began, and when the two sets of population in Worcester settled down to a better neighborhood acquaintance, the inevitable antipathies waked up as between Englishmen and Scotchmen, as between Presbyterians and Puritans. Certain traits and habits of our folks, to be specified later as common to them in all New England, intensified the feeling of repugnance felt toward them in Worcester. They were commonly called "Irish." Even a formal act of the General Court of Massachusetts denominated them "poor Irish people"; and a little later the General Court of New Hampshire styled the Londonderry section of them "a company of Irish at Nutfield." This designation they all naturally enough resented. "We are surprised," writes Rev. James McGregor, the pastor of Londonderry, in a letter to Governor Shute, bearing date in 1720, "to hear ourselves termed Irish people, when we so frequently ventured our all for the British crown and liberties against the Irish papists, and gave all tests of our loyalty which the government of Ireland required, and are always ready to do the same when required."

In Worcester there were at least two, Abraham Blair and William Caldwell, and in Londonderry several more, including Rev. Matthew Clark, of the survivors of the heroic defense of the Ulster Londonderry in 1689; and these men and their heirs were made free of taxation throughout the British provinces by Act of Parliament, and occupied what were called "*exempt farms*" in New England until the American Revolution, so immensely important to the establishment of their throne did William and Mary hold the services of the Protestant settlers and defenders of Ulster against the last and the worst of the Stuarts. Now, for these very men and their companions in exile to be stigmatized as "Irish," in the sense in which that term was then held in reproach, was a bitter pill to our fathers; and this, and other prejudices more or less well-founded, only yielded, in the course of time, to the influence of their simple virtues and sterling worth.

The tenure by which these people held their lands in Worcester seems at first to have been the same as that of their English neighbors, who came earlier; namely, by direct grant of the General Court of Massachusetts: at any rate, there is a very early record that lots were so granted to John Gray and Andrew McFarland, two of their leaders; and the lots so granted earlier to members of the Committee of Settlement, and to others not actual settlers, were soon in the market at a very cheap price, and it is known that some of the families bought these lots at second hand, because the deeds are on record, and I have seen them; it was not, accordingly, at this point, of lands or anything connected with them, that the jealousy and bitterness between the two strains of blood began, but rather at the point of differences of language and personal habits, and especially of church beliefs and ceremonial. The English had put up a rude log meeting-house the year before the Scotch-Irish came, and the year after a more commodious structure was erected on the site of the "Old South Church" (but quite recently removed); the Ulster Presbyterians, from the very first, liked to have worship by themselves, and in their own way, whenever and wherever they could; it is known that they held service, sometimes in summer, in the open air, and for a considerable period, by vote of the town, they occupied for preaching purposes one of the old garrison houses, commonly called the "Old Fort." Here having formed a religious society, they enjoyed for a time the ministrations of Rev. Edward Fitzgerald and Rev. William Johnston; still, they did not abandon the Puritan Church on the Common, and were taxed, of course, for its support. This taxation made friction, for they were poor and could not support their own minister besides contributing to the support of the other; and Mr. Fitzgerald, being unable to procure proper maintenance, removed from the town. The numbers of Presbyterian communicants were nearly equal to those of the Congregational Church, and the latter had proposed a union with the former; and Mr. Fitzgerald had once been invited to occupy the pulpit, vacated by the dismissal of Rev. Mr. Gardner in 1722, for a single Sabbath when no candidate could be procured, but the request was not repeated, and no inducement was held out to him to remain.

In 1725 the English settled a new minister in the person of Rev. Isaac Burr, and the tacit understanding if not the express agreement was that if the Presbyterians would aid morally and pecuniarily in his support, they should be permitted to place in the pulpit occasionally teachers of their own denomination; and so the Scotch people united with the other inhabitants. After some time, finding that their expectations were not being realized in this regard, and were not likely to be, the Scotch withdrew from the Church on the Common, and installed the Rev. William Johnston to be their minister. Feelings were deepening, difficulties in the way of union were multiplying, and the Scotch had no suitable place of worship of their own. When, in 1733, the Church on the Common was repaired and somewhat adorned, and a committee of seven (all English) being appointed "to seat ye meeting-house pursuant to instructions," it cannot be denied that the olive-branch was held out to the party of the second part by assigning them in general very good seats, according to the standard of the time; for example : "In ye fore section of ye body" (with five English families), John Gray ; "In ye second section of ye body" (with three English), William Gray, James Hamilton, Andrew McFarland, John Clark, Robert Peebles ; "In ye third section of ye body" (all Scotch), Matthew Gray, Alexander McKonkey, William Caldwell, John Duncan, William Gray, Jr., Matthew Gray, Jr., Andrew McFarland, Jr., John Gray, Jr. ; "In ye fourth section of ye body" (with four English), James Thornington, John Battey, Oliver Wallis, Robert Blair ; "In ye fifth section of ye body" (all Scotch), James Forbush, John Alexander, William Mahan, John Stimson, Duncan Graham, John McFarland, Joseph Clark ; "In ye sixth section of ye body" (with three English families), John Patrick, James Glasford, John Sterling, Hugh Kelso ; "In ye fore section of ye foremost gallery" (no Scotch) ; "In ye second section of ye foremost gallery" (with five English), Samuel Gray, Thomas Hamilton, Matthew Clark, William Temple ; "In ye fore section of ye long gallery" (with fourteen English), William McClellan, James McClellan, John Cishiel, Robert Barbour ; "In ye second section in ye long gallery" (with three English), Patrick Peebles, John McKonkey, Robert Marble, John Peebles.

Three years after this apparently ostentatious patronage of the Presbyterians, the latter, having been compelled to contribute for eleven years to the support of the Rev. Mr. Burr without any pulpit or other recognition of their peculiar views, made a formal appeal to the justice of their fellow-townsmen in town meeting for relief from a tax inconsistent with their religious privileges. It was of no avail. The petition is not extant, since little care was taken to preserve the memorials of this unoffending but persecuted people, whose history discloses the injustice and intolerance of our English ancestors ; but the answer of the town of Worcester to their application is on record, and it is a curious specimen of an attempt to make the worse appear the better reason. One can hardly say whether there be in it more of Yankee subtlety or religious illiberality. It begins in this way : "In answer to the petition of John Clark and others, praying to be released from paying toward the support of the Rev. Isaac Burr, pastor of the church in this town, or any other except Mr. Johnston, the town, upon mature consideration, think that the request is unreasonable, and that they ought not to comply

with it, upon many considerations." Thereupon follow four enumerated and elaborate alleged reasons for refusal, no one of them,
nor all of them together, expressing fully the real reasons. The
first is a mere quibble; the second asserts that, inasmuch as both
churches follow substantially the Westminster Confession of Faith,
"they may enjoy the same worship, ordinances, and Christian privileges, and means of their spiritual edification, with us, as in the
way which they call Presbyterian, and their consciences not be
imposed on in anything." As is usual in this kind of document,
the third enumerated consideration falls into an accusing of the
brethren, "but we have rather reason to suppose that their separation
from us is from some irregular views and motives, which it would
be unworthy of us to countenance"; and the fourth consideration I
will quote in full, for the purpose of exhibiting its spirit: "We
look upon the petitioners and others breaking off from us as they
have done, as being full of irregularity and disorder, not to mention
that the ordination of their minister was disorderly, even with
respect to the principles which they themselves pretend to act by,
as well as with respect to us, to whom they stand related, and with
whom they cohabit, and enjoy with us in common all proper social,
civil, and Christian rights and privileges; their separating from us
being contrary to the public establishment and laws of this Province;
contrary to their own covenant with us, and unreasonably weaken-
ing to the town, whose numbers and dimensions (the north part
being excepted by the vote from paying to Mr. Burr) will not admit
of the honorable support of two ministers of the gospel, and tending
to cause and cherish divisions and parties, greatly destructive to
our civil and religious interests, and the peace, tranquillity, and
happiness."

It is hardly necessary to add that these masterful bits of logic,
from which almost all of the formal fallacies of the books might be
illustrated, carried the town by a large majority. This was in 1736.
It gave rise to two distinct impulses among the Presbyterians: first,
to build a meeting-house of their own, in which "Mr. Johnston"
might officiate, which there was no law to prevent; and second,
among individuals of better fortune and more independence than
the rest, to shake off the dust of their feet for a testimony against
the infinitesimal bigotry of Worcester Puritans, and go elsewhere.

The Worcester Registry of Deeds bears ample evidence that
many farms in the "north part" of the town, where the Scotch-Irish
were specially located, and where the "Old Fort" stood in which
they sometimes worshiped, changed hands in 1737, and in the years

immediately following.   John Gray, for example, and each of three
sons of his, made significant conveyances of land in Worcester in
that interval; and it is quite noticeable that the name of John
Clark, the first to sign the petition to the town of Worcester for
exemption from church taxes in behalf of himself and fellow signers,
stands prominent a couple of years later among the first settlers of
the Scotch-Irish town of Colerain, fifty miles to the northwest
of Worcester, so named from the old Ulster town on the Bann.
The Morrisons, Pennells, Herrouns, Hendersons, Cochranes, Hunters,
Henrys, Clarks, McClellans, McCowens, Taggarts, and McDowells,
many of whom had been previous settlers in Worcester, were the
chief families in this frontier and Presbyterian town, now on the
border of Vermont.

But the most striking proof of the discontent of the folks of our
blood with their church-treatment in Worcester was the formal
organization there in 1738, two years after the contemptuous rejec-
tion of their petition, of a company consisting of thirty-four families
to purchase and settle a new town on principles in keeping with
their own.   Thus originated Pelham, about thirty miles west of
Worcester.   Robert Peebles and James Thornington (afterward
spelled Thornton) were a committee to contract with Colonel John
Stoddard and others, who owned the territory.   In the contract
occurs this passage: "It is agreed that families of good connection
be settled on the premises, who shall be such as were the inhabitants
of the Kingdom of Ireland or their descendants, being Protestants,
and none to be admitted but such as bring good and undeniable
credentials or certificates of their being persons of good conversation
and of the Presbyterian persuasion as used in the Church of Scotland, and conform to the discipline thereof."

The first meeting of these proprietors was held in Worcester at
the house of Captain Daniel Haywood in February, 1739, and all
subsequent meetings of the proprietors were held in Worcester, until
in August, 1740, when a meeting was held in the new township at
the house of John Ferguson.   At this first meeting in their own
new town it was "voted to build a meeting-house, to raise £100
towards building it, and choose a committee to agree with a work-
man to raise the house and provide for the settling of a minister."
Subsequent to this, £220 were raised in two installments for the
erection and completion of the structure.   In the spring of 1743
two meetings were held in the new meeting-house, and measures
were then taken "to glaze the meeting-house, to build a pulpit, and
underpin the house at the charge of the town."   The first pastor

they called to settle was their old quasi-pastor at Worcester, Rev. Mr. Johnston, who had in the meantime removed to Londonderry, N. H.; but he naturally enough declined the call. But Robert Abercrombie, a native of Edinburgh, a profound scholar, and possessor of a library surpassed by few in its time, and which has been kept together till the present time, began to preach to the people in the summer of 1742. His ordination sermon was preached by the famous Jonathan Edwards, and he remained a steadfast friend and coadjutor of that persecuted servant of God throughout his subsequent troubles in the neighboring Northampton. It is worth noting that the public school of Pelham was kept in the new meeting-house for about ten years, when it was "voted to build three school-houses, one at the Meeting-house, one at the West End of the town, and one on the East Hill."

Now, notwithstanding these repeated drafts on the home colony and church at Worcester, to Colerain and Pelham and elsewhere, those who remained there were still determined to build a meeting-house of their own. They had been weakened, but not disheartened. They naturally chose a site near to the "Old Fort," which had been to them more or less a worshiping-place, on the "Boston road," not far from the center of their scattered homesteads. I have often been in the neighborhood of this place, and am confident I can point out the spot within a very few rods. In their extreme poverty they raised the needful moneys, the timber was brought to the site, framed and raised, and the building in the earlier progress of construction, when the other inhabitants of Worcester, many of them persons of consideration and respectability and professed piety, gathered tumultuously in the night-time, leveled the structure with the ground, sawed the timbers, and burnt or carried off the pieces and other materials. This was in 1740. The defenseless, but indignant strangers were compelled to submit to this infamous wrong. The English Puritans and their irresponsible hangers-on chose, indeed, the night-time for their mob-violence and devilish meanness, but no blackness of darkness can ever cover up a deed like this; no sophistries, no neighborhood mis-affinities, no town votes, no race jealousies, no wretched shibboleth of any name, can ever wipe out that stain. The blood of English Puritans and of Scotch Presbyterians mingles in my veins; my great-grandfather Perry, my grandfather of the same name, my uncle, too, in the same line, officiated as deacons for ninety-four successive years in the old South Church on the Common, which originated and perpetrated this outrage on humanity; nevertheless, I give my feeble word of utter condemnation for this shameless act of bigotry, the details of which I learned as a little boy at my mother's knee.

The motives to a still further exodus from Worcester on the part of the Scotch were of course still further intensified by this scandalous destruction of their property in 1740, and it is significant, that the third and fourth purely Scotch-Irish towns in Massachusetts, namely, Western (now Warren), in Worcester County, and Blandford, in Hampden County, were both incorporated the next year, 1741. These two towns, even more than the two earlier ones, Pelham and Colerain, have continued and still remain in the hands of the descendants of the Worcester families. In Blandford the families of Blair, Boise, Knox, Carnahan, Watson, Wilson, and Ferguson were prominent; and in Western some of the same names, especially the Blairs, with Reeds and Crawfords, and many more. Notwithstanding these successive migrations from Worcester, a very considerable number of families remained there; among them, the McClellans, the Caldwells, the Blairs, the McFarlands, the Rankins, the Grays, the Crawfords, the Youngs, the Hamiltons, the Duncans, the Grahams, the Forbushes, the Kelsos, the Clarks, the Fergusons, the McClintocks, the McKonkeys, the Glasfords, and the McGregors. The later movement of individual families from Worcester and Pelham and Colerain and Western and Blandford carried Scotch-Irish blood into every town of Western Massachusetts, and ultimately into most of the towns of Vermont, while the reflex movement from and into Massachusetts to and from the contemporary settlements in New Hampshire and Maine, soon to be characterized, served to keep in touch and sympathy, in mutual acquaintance and interchange of ministers, and more or less of intermarriage, all these local centers of our race in New England.

The two most distinguished men who have come out from this Worcester branch of the great migration of 1718, have been Dr. Matthew Thornton, a signer of the Declaration of Independence, and Professor Asa Gray, at the time of his death the most accomplished botanist in the world.

Matthew Thornton (or Thornington, as the name was then spelled) was a lad of four years when the five ships zigzagged into Boston Harbor. His father, James Thornton, instead of going to Worcester directly that autumn, was one of a company — Willis estimates them at about three hundred — who wintered on shipboard in Portland Harbor. In the spring, with few others, he settled at Wiscasset, in the Kennebec country. After a very few years there, we find both father and son in Worcester, where the boy received whatever primary education he had, and after studying medicine, which was rudely taught in those days, commenced practice in Londonderry, among those who were from his native land, and who proverbially possess warm national remembrances. Here he acquired a wide reputation as a physician, and in the course of several years of successful practice became comparatively rich for those times. He also sustained several public offices, taking, as Scotch-Irishmen are wont to do, an active and influential part in the public affairs of his locality.

He became surgeon to a regiment of New Hampshire men in the famous expedition against Cape Breton under Pepperell in 1745; and it is related of his regiment of five hundred men that only six died previously to the surrender of Louisburg, although a company from Londonderry commanded by Captain John Mooar, were employed for fourteen successive nights, with straps over their shoulders, and sinking to their knees in mud, in drawing cannon from the landing-place to the camp, through a morass. Scotch-Irishmen always hated the French next to the Devil!

At the breaking out of the Revolution, Thornton held the post of colonel in the New Hampshire militia, and had also been commissioned a justice of the peace by Benning Wentworth, acting under British authority; but after Lexington and Concord, on the 19th of April, 1775, John Wentworth, then governor, retired from the government of New Hampshire and went to England. Under these circumstances the colony called a "Provincial Convention," of which Thornton was appointed president. There was no state constitution as yet, and no declaration of independence, but there was no other constituted government in the province besides this provincial convention, and I am fond of thinking, and believe it to be historically correct to affirm, that this extemporized but indispensable New Hampshire convention, presided over by a Scotch-Irishman, Ulster-born, was the first independent sovereignty upon this continent! It certainly assumed the functions of an independent government in the name of the people of the Colony.

Thereafter the public career of Matthew Thornton, both in state and nation, is well known to the world; and a station on the Railroad from Boston to Concord commemorates in its name, "Thornton's Ferry," a fine estate on the banks of the Merrimac, confiscated by New Hampshire from its then Tory owner, which later became by purchase the home and last resting-place of the first of our kith and kin to gain a national reputation here in the line of statesmanship.

An anecdote of Judge Thornton has been preserved which may

serve to illustrate the keen and ready wit possessed by him in
common with most of the Scotch-Irish race. In his old age, 1798,
he happened to attend a session of the New Hampshire legislature,
which met in a town adjoining his own. He was eighty-four years
old. He had served many years before in all three branches of the
legislature. Meeting at this time an old Londonderry neighbor,
who was now a member of the House, the latter asked the judge if
he did not think the legislature had improved very much since the
old days when he held a seat? if it did not have more men of natural
and acquired abilities, and more eloquent speakers than formerly,
"for then," said he, "you know that there were but five or six who
could make speeches, but now all we farmers can make speeches."
"To answer that question, I will tell you a story I remember to
have heard related of an old gentleman, a farmer, who lived but a
short distance from my father's residence in Ireland. This old
gentleman was very exemplary in his observance of religious duties,
and made it a constant practice to read a portion of Scripture
morning and evening before addressing the Throne of Grace. It
happened one morning that he was reading the chapter which gives
an account of Samson catching three hundred foxes, when the old
lady, his wife, interrupted him by saying, 'John, I'm sure that
canna' be true; for our Isaac was as good a fox-hunter as there ever
was in the country, and he never caught but about twenty.' 'Hooh!
Janet,' replied the old gentleman, 'ye mauna' always tak' the
Scripture just as it reads; perhaps in the three hundred there might
ha' been aughteen, or may be twanty, that were real foxes; the rest
were all skunks and woodchucks.' "

Professor Asa Gray, the cosmopolitan botanist, was born in Paris,
N. Y., in 1810, and died in his seventy-eighth year, in Cambridge,
the seat of his labors and the center of his fame. He was a great-
great-grandson of the first Matthew Gray of Worcester, to whom I
also stand in the same genealogical relation. Some ten years ago
I spent, by invitation, an evening at his house, in order to unfold to
him a little the story of our common ancestors in Worcester. He
was very courteous, and apparently attentive; but I soon discovered
that the drift and training of his mind had led him to care vastly
more about the genealogy and physiology of plants the world over
than about the genealogy and mode of life of that Scotch-Irish
ancestry from whom, nevertheless, he derived directly all the peculiar
traits of his own mental activity. He was canny, absorbed, analytic,
comprehensive, religiously consecrated.

In 1885, on attaining his seventy-fifth year, he was the recipient of a large and beautiful silver vase, the gift of the botanists of the United States to their honored master, and a flood of congratulations from friends at home and abroad. The following terse and appropriate lines were sent by James Russell Lowell:

> " Kind Fate, prolong the days well spent,
>   Whose indefatigable hours
> Have been as gaily innocent
> And fragrant as his flowers."

Comparatively early in life he became a member of most of the learned societies of the world, and at length even the most exclusive gladly opened their doors to him. The Royal Society of London was one of these, and he was also one of the " immortal eight" foreign members of the French Institute. During his last visit to Europe, the last summer of his life, he was received with distinguished honors everywhere, among which were the highest degrees ever conferred by the great universities of Oxford, Cambridge, and Edinburgh.

He himself tersely and modestly stated his own fundamental beliefs as follows: "I am, scientifically and in my own fashion, a Darwinian; philosophically, a convinced Theist; and religiously, an accepter of the creed commonly called the Nicene, as the exponent of the Christian faith."

2. LONDONDERRY. The core of the company that settled Londonderry, N. H., in April, 1719, consisted of sixteen men, with their families, namely: James McKeen, John Barnett, Archibald Clendenin, John Mitchell, James Sterrett, James Anderson, Randall Alexander, James Gregg, James Clark, James Nesmith, Allen Anderson, Robert Weir, John Morrison, Samuel Allison, Thomas Steele, John Stuart. Thirteen of these men lived to an average age of seventy-nine years; six of them attained to nearly ninety, and two of them overpassed that limit; and one, John Morrison, lived to see ninety-seven years. All of the Scotch-Irish of that generation, wherever they located in New England, unless their personal habits were such as shorten life, attained on the average to a very advanced age. The pioneers in this second settlement were most of them men in middle life, robust and persevering, and adventurous and strong-willed, fronting death with no thought of surrender. Most of them were the descendants of Scotch Covenanters who had passed over to Ulster later than the mass of the settlers there; and they had kept together in church relations, as well as in residence, more closely than most of the Scotch settlers. Their residence was in

the valley of the Bann, mostly on the Antrim side of the river, in or near the towns or parishes of Coleraine, Ballymoney, Ballymena, Ballywatick, and Kilrea; and when they decided to emigrate, they still wished to keep together in church relations; and those of them who had been under the pastoral charge of Rev. James McGregor, who came with them, especially the McKeen families and their numerous connections, desired to form a distinct settlement here and become again the charge of their beloved pastor.

With this end in view, about twenty families, taking others with them, amounting in all (as Willis estimated) to three hundred persons, sailed from Boston in the late autumn to explore Casco Bay for a home, under a promise from Governor Shute of a grant of land whenever and wherever they decided upon a location in any still unappropriated quarter in New England. They wintered, hungry and cold, in Portland harbor. In the early spring they explored to the eastward, but there is no record how far they went or what they found. It is enough for our present purpose that Maine seemed to offer no genial home to those sea-worn and weather-beaten voyagers. Though they left a few of their number in Portland, to whom we shall recur later, and probably a larger number on the Kennebec at or near Wiscasset, the bulk determined to seek a milder climate and a more favorable location. Undoubtedly, while still in Boston their attention had been called to Southern New Hampshire as well as to Maine, both at that time under the jurisdiction of the governor of Massachusetts, for they sailed directly back to the mouth of the Merrimac and anchored at Haverhill, on that river, where they heard of a fine tract of land about fifteen miles to the northward, then called Nutfield, on account of the abundance of the chestnut and walnut and butternut trees which, in connection with the pines, distinguished the growth of its forests. A party, under the lead of James McKeen, grandfather of the first president of Bowdoin College, and brother-in-law of Pastor McGregor, went up and examined the tract; and ascertaining that it was not appropriated, they decided at once to take up here the grant obtained from the government of Massachusetts of a township twelve miles square of any of her unappropriated lands.

Having selected the spot on which to commence their settlement, and having built a few temporary huts on a little brook which they called "West-Running Brook," a tributary of Beaver Brook, which falls into the Merrimac at Lowell, and leaving two or three of their number in charge, they returned to Haverhill to bring on their families, their provisions, their implements of labor, and household

utensils. Mr. McGregor and some others had passed the winter at
Dracut, on Beaver Brook, just north of Lowell; and two parties,
one from Dracut and the other from Haverhill, were soon converging
through the forests toward West-Running Brook, when they met,
as tradition says, at a place ever after called "Horse Hill," from
the fact that both parties there tied their horses while the men
surveyed the territory around as the future home. This day was
April 11, old style, 1719. The next day, having in the meantime
explored with the leaders more fully what they had selected for the
township, the good pastor, under a large oak on the east side of
Beaver Pond, delivered to his people, now partially re-united, the
first sermon ever preached in that region — Isaiah 32, 2: "And a
man shall be as a hiding-place from the wind, and a covert from the
tempest; as rivers of water in a dry place; as the shadow of a
great rock in a weary land." The spot where this religious service
was held, especially the tree around which these hardy pioneers
assembled, was for a long period regarded with great reverence by
the people of Londonderry. When at last it decayed and fell, the
owner of the field in which it stood planted a young apple tree
among its rotten roots, which now serves, and will long serve, to
designate the venerated spot.

These first families, in order to secure the advantages of near
neighborhood, and be better able to protect themselves against the
attacks of the Indians, with which all the New England colonies
were at that time threatened, planted their log-houses on each side
of West-Running Brook, on home-lots but thirty rods wide and
extending back on a north and south line till they inclosed sixty
acres each. These lots constituted what has ever since been called
the Double Range. For fifty years or more this range continued
to be a populous section of the town. The first season the settlers
cultivated a field alongside the brook, then and ever since called the
"Common Field"; but the best land in the township was not in
that section, for it lay too low, and as each settler had allotted to
him another sixty acres elsewhere, after a while the lowland began
to be deserted of houses, and nothing is now to be seen along the
Double Range but meadows, dotted here and there by the cellar-holes
of these earliest planters. No price was paid for the land, since it
was the free gift of King William to his loyal subjects of the old
country, some of them faithful champions of his throne in the siege
and defense of Londonderry.

The first dwellings were, of course, of logs, and covered with
bark. It is to be noticed, however, that in these exiles for right-

eousness' sake, sound and pious as they were, there was as much human nature to the square inch as in the rest of mankind. When John Morrison was building his house in the Double Range his wife came to him, and in a persuasive, affectionate manner said to him, "Aweel, aweel, dear Joan, an' it maun be a log-house, do make it a log heegher nor the lave" (than the rest). Beaver Brook, however, tumbles well in its course from the pond to the Merrimac, and saw-mills were soon built, and within a year or two good framed houses were erected; the first for Pastor McGregor, only quite recently demolished, and the second by John McMurphy, Esq., who bore a commission as justice of the peace, dated in Ireland, and so antedated the commission signed by Governor Shute, April 29, 1720, to Justice James McKeen, in some sense the foremost man of the settlement.

Two stone garrison-houses, strongly built and well prepared to resist an attack of the Indians, were put up the first season; and to these the several families retired at night whenever, for any reason, special danger from that source was apprehended. But it is remarkable that neither in Lovell's War, when Londonderry was strictly a frontier town, nor in either of the two subsequent French and Indian wars, did any hostile force from the northward ever even approach that town. Tradition has always been busy in ascribing the signal preservation of this colony from the attacks of the Indians to the influence of Pastor McGregor over Governor Vaudreuil of Canada. It is said that they had known each other in the Old World at college; that a correspondence was kept up between them on this side the water; that at the request of his friend the governor caused means to be used for the protection of the settlement; that he induced the Catholic priests to charge the Indians not to injure any of these people, as they were different from the English, and that the warriors were assured beforehand that no bounty would be paid for such scalps, and no sins forgiven to those who killed them. It is certain that the early inhabitants of Londonderry believed in all these assertions; and it is some confirmation of them that a manuscript sermon of McGregor's, still extant, has on the margin the name and various titles of the Marquis Vaudreuil, by which, of course, he would be addressed upon occasion.

At any rate, the earliest pioneers were much indebted to the volunteer services of an Indian of some tribe and connection. Taking Mr. McGregor to a high hill, he pointed to a tall pine some nine miles distant, and told him that in that direction and neighborhood there were falls in the river, where he would find an abundance of fish. By the help of his compass the pastor, with a few of the settlers, was able to mark out a course to Amoskeag Falls, where the city of Manchester now stands, and with a scoop-net, which they had provided, readily secured an ample supply of salmon and shad, with which the Merrimac then abounded. This was for a long time a valuable resource to the inhabitants of Londonderry. The salted fish constituted an important article of their food, especially before their new fields became productive. But their food at best was scant and poor for many years. Bean porridge, barley broth, hasty pudding, samp and potatoes, were the chief reliance.

In securing a perfectly valid title to their lands, and the democratic privileges of a town corporate, the people of Londonderry experienced no little embarrassment. The executive jurisdiction of Governor Shute over the territory was acknowledged by everybody, and the validity of his grant to them of the land in the king's name; but could they also get a prior title direct from the original Indian chiefs claiming to own the land? Rev. John Wheelright of Exeter had obtained by fair purchase, in 1629, from the four principal Sagamores, all the territory lying between the river Piscataqua and the Merrimac. Colonel John Wheelright of Wells, Me., had inherited from his grandfather that portion of this right now occupied by the Scotch-Irish; and he gave to a committee of these, partly at the instance of Lieutenant-Governor Wentworth of New Hampshire, a formal deed of the land ten miles square, corresponding to the grant of Governor Shute; and in consideration of this service both Wheelright and Wentworth received certain lots of land in Londonderry, which proved in the sequel to be some of the best farms in the town.

Before this was accomplished, however, appeared the first state paper of the Scotch-Irish in America, the original of which is now among the collections of the New Hampshire Historical Society, which I proceed to quote in full, because it shows there were men among them — probably in this case James Gregg and Robert Wear, who signed it — who knew how to put sharp points into clean words, and especially because it shows that they thoroughly appreciated already the town-government system of New England, and wanted all its advantages for themselves:

"The humble petition of the people late from Ireland, now settled at Nutfield, to His Excellency the Governour and General Court assembled at Portsmouth, Sept. 23, 1719, — Humbly sheweth: That your petitioners having made application to the General Court

met at Boston in October last, and having obtained a grant for a
township in any part of their unappropriated lands, took encouragement thereupon to settle at Nutfield about the Eleventh of April
last, which is situated by estimation about fourteen miles from
Haverel meeting-house to the North-west, and about fifteen miles
from Dracut meeting-house on the River Merrimack north and
by east.   That your petitioners since their settlement have found
that the said Nutfield is claimed by three or four different parties
by virtue of Indian deeds, yet none of them offered any dis-
turbance to your petitioners except one party from Newbury and
Salem.   Their deed from one John, Indian, bears date March 13,
Anno Dom. 1701, and imparts that they had made a purchase of
said land for five pounds.   By virtue of this deed they claim ten
miles square westward from Heverel line ; and one Caleb Moody of
Newbury, in their name, discharged our people from clearing or any
way improving the said land, unless we agreed that 20 or 25 families
at most should dwell there, and that all the rest of the land should
be reserved for them.   That your petitioners by reading the grant
of the Crown of Great Britain to the Province of Massachusetts Bay,
which determineth their northern line three miles from the River
Merrimack from any and every part of the River, and by advice
from such as were more capable to judge of this affair are satisfied that the said Nutfield is within his majesties province of New
Hampshire, which we are further confirmed in, because the General
Court met at Boston in May last upon our renewed application, did
not think fit any way to intermeddle with the said land.   That your
petitioners, therefore, embrace this opportunity of addressing this
Honorable Court, praying that their township may consist of ten
miles square, or in a figure equivalent to it, they being in number
about seventy families and inhabitants, and more of their friends
arrived from Ireland to settle with them, and many of the people
of New England settling with them ; and that they being so numerous, may be erected into a township with its usual privileges,
and have a power of making town officers and laws.   That, being a
frontier place, they may the better subsist by government amongst
them, and may be more strong and full of inhabitants.   That your
petitioners being descended from, and professing the faith and
principles of, the established Church of North Britain, and loyal
subjects of the British Crown in the family of his majesty King
George, and encouraged by the happy administration of his majesties
chief governour in these provinces [Gov. Shute], and the favorable
inclination of the good people of New England to their brethren,

adventuring to come over and plant in this vast wilderness, humbly expect a favorable answer from this Honourable Court, and your petitioners as in duty bound shall ever pray, etc. Subscribed at Nutfield in the name of our people, Sept. 21, 1719."

Under the auspices, perhaps it would be proper to say patronage, of Lieutenant-Governor Wentworth, Nutfield was incorporated as a town in June, 1722, containing ten square miles indeed, but not equilateral, "duly bounded," panhandled, gerrymandered, so as to reach up to their fishing station on the Merrimac at Amoskeag Falls — this portion afterward called Derryfield, and now Manchester. The following entry upon the town record must not only be viewed as a genuine token of gratitude for past favors received, but also in part as expressing a sense of pre-thankfulness for "the substance of things hoped for": "The people of Nutfield do acknowledge with gratitude the obligation they are under to the Hon. John Wentworth, Esq., Lieutenant-Governor of New Hampshire. They remember with pleasure, that His Honor, on all occasions, showed a great deal of civility and real kindness to them, being strangers in the country, and cherished the small beginnings of their settlement and defended them from the encroachment and violence of such as upon unjust grounds would have disturbed their settlement, and always gave them a favorable ear and easy access to government, and procured justice for them, and established order, and promoted peace and good government amongst them; giving them always the most wholesome and seasonable advice, both with respect to the purity and liberty of the gospel, and the management of their secular concerns, and put arms and ammunition into their hands to defend them from the fears and dangers of the Indians; and contributed liberally, by his influence and example, to the building of a house for the worship of God; so that, under God, we own him for the patron and guardian of our settlement, and erect this monument of gratitude to the name and family of Wentworth, to be had in the greatest veneration by the present generation and the latest posterity."

In the meantime and afterward, the people of the town now christened Londonderry at its incorporation, though the ancestors of most of them came from the parallel valley dividing County Antrim from County Londonderry, — the siege and defense of the Ulster town in which some of them had taken a personal part giving that name the preference, — were surveying their heritage, building their first meeting-house, and laying out upon the higher grounds new ranges for farms. Among the first of these was the English

Range, so-called, to accommodate a few heads of families from Massachusetts who had cast in their lot with, and were welcomed by, the Scotch-Irish. Number One on the English Range was assigned to Joseph Simonds, who was one of the first twenty heads of families, who was one of the four undertakers to build in 1719 the first saw-mill on Beaver Brook, and who (which is much less worth the mention) was one of the great-great-great-grandfathers of my children. A few weeks ago I had myself driven leisurely in a buggy over all parts of ancient Londonderry; I crossed the original farm of Joseph Simonds, No. 1 in the English Range, and was told by Mr. Choate, proprietor of the same or adjoining estate, that "the best lands in Londonderry were on the English Range"; I rode, also, over the crest of Aiken's Range, and along the brook bearing the same name, and farther west toward the so-called High Range, past the second-built church, and then bearing east past the site of Dr. Morrison's church, and near the place of the Hill church and graveyard, and, crossing the railroad again, with Beaver Pond on the left, climbed the hill past the original meeting-house, which John Wentworth helped to build, and the original graveyard there, — God's own sown field, — and on the road towards Parson Mc-Gregor's first framed house, touched the highest land in old Londonderry; whence returning to Derry village, we crossed the old "West-Running Brook," and passed also by the "Common Field," and on Beaver Brook again, the place of the first saw-mill, which Joseph Simonds helped to build, and where logs have been rolled in and boards tossed out from that day to this.

It was not all harmony in state or church in ancient Londonderry. The town thrived and the congregation became very large. "Many men of many minds." The Scotch-Irish were a straight-thinking and a plain-speaking people. Parson McGregor died in 1729. Though but a youth at the time, he took part in the defense of the Ulster Derry, and always claimed to have himself discharged the large guns from the tower of the cathedral which announced to the starving besieged below the approach of the ships up the Foyle that brought them the final relief. Soon after the death of McGregor, Rev. Matthew Clark, then seventy years old, came direct from Ireland to Londonderry, and was asked to supply the desk and take pastoral care, but not to become formal pastor. There is extant an original portrait of this man, representing him with a black patch around the outer angle of the right eye, the patch covering a wound that refused to heal, received in one of the sallies of the besieged at Londonderry. He had been an officer in the Protestant army during the civil commotions in King William's time, and had been particularly active in the defense of Derry. It is related of him that, while sitting as moderator of the presbytery, the martial music of a training band passing by recalled the smoldering fires of his youth, and made him incapable for a little time to attend to his duties, and his reply to the repeated calls of the brethren was, "Nae business while I hear the toot o' the drum!" and when he died at the age of seventy-six, in January, 1735, in compliance with his special request on his death-bed, his remains were borne to the grave by those only who had been his fellow-soldiers and fellow-sufferers in the siege of Londonderry! This is at once the most picturesque and the most pathetic scene in the story of the Scotch-Irish in New England. Forty-five years after the event, this modern Israel, this "Warrior of God," in two senses, borne along between the mingled pines and nut-trees of a new God's acre in the wilderness, by those only who, with him, had stood to the outermost verge of their lives for the faith once delivered to the saints!

Two years after the death of Matthew Clark, David McGregor, son of the first minister, who had received his literary and theological education chiefly under the tuition of Clark, himself an university-bred man, took pastoral charge of the new West Parish in Londonderry. Two meeting-houses had already been built in this parish —one on Aiken's Range, and the other, called the Hill Meeting-house, nearly a mile west. Here were the seeds of a deep-seated and long-continued quarrel. Moreover, there was great dissatisfaction with Mr. Davidson, the third pastor in the old parish. The population was increasing, and was already beginning to diffuse itself into new settlements in the neighborhood. At a sacramental season in 1734, only fifteen years from the first settlement, there were present, according to the church records, seven hundred communicants. The everlasting place-of-the-meeting-house question, which has wrought more plague and alienation in New England than all theological dogmas put together, was stirring up the ministers and the sessions and the people into a hotch-potch; and this, as at Worcester, with other matters of disagreement, intensified the spirit of separation, and multiplied in course of time new colonies going forth to post themselves elsewhere. During the quarter-century preceding the Revolution, ten distinct settlements were made by emigrants from Londonderry, all of which became towns of influence and importance in New Hampshire. Two strong townships in Vermont, and two in Nova Scotia, were settled from the same source within the same time; besides which, numerous families, sometimes singly and sometimes in groups, went off in all directions, especially northward and westward, up the Connecticut River and over the ridge of the Green Mountains, to carry everywhere the sturdy qualities, the fixed opinions, and the lasting grudges characteristic of Scotch-Irishmen.

Neither the crown nor the colonies ever appealed in vain to these brave people, now widely scattered, for help in the old French wars. Not a route to Ticonderoga or Crown Point but was tramped again and again by the firm-set feet of these New England Protestants. They were with Colonel Williams in the "bloody morning scout" at the head of Lake George in 1755, and in the battle with Dieskau that followed; they were with Stark and Lord Howe under Abercrombie in the terrible defeat at Ticonderoga in 1758; many of them toiled under General Amherst at his great stone fort at Crown Point in 1759, whose broken ruins even astound us to-day; and others still were with General Wolfe on the Heights of Abraham the same year, where and when was fought the most vital and decisive battle ever seen upon this continent. Major Robert Rogers, the famous commander of the three companies of rangers raised by New Hampshire in 1756, was himself a native of Londonderry, and most of his men were enlisted in the same locality.

When it came to the Revolution, however, Rogers's loyalty to the English king, for whom he had risked his life in numberless scouts and fights, overrode his sense of the grievance of the colonies, and he was proscribed as a Tory by the act of New Hampshire. Not so John Stark. Stark was captain of one of Rogers's companies of rangers, and at one time commanded the whole corps, with the rank of major. Rogers went to England in 1777, and Stark, the same year, went to Bennington! In August next will be consecrated there, with fitting ceremonial, to national and local liberty, a limestone shaft three hundred and one feet high, whose foundations are cut into the solid and everlasting rock — a shaft paid for from out the treasuries of the three states which furnished Stark his men for that fight; from out the treasury of the United States, under whose colors, a little later, he fought Burgoyne in person at Saratoga, and from out the scattered contributions of patriotic men and women all over the land; a shaft which will stand a silent witness for many things and many men — for the Berkshire militia, for the Green Mountain Boys and the Catamount tavern, but most of all for John Stark, the most distinguished Scotch-Irishman of New England, a native of Londonderry, and for the seventy Derry volunteers who went with him to Bennington, and whose names are of record, and for Robert McGregor, a grandson of the old pastor, who was on Stark's staff in 1777!

Colonel George Reid, another native of Londonderry, pure blood, held a command in the New Hampshire forces during the entire war of the Revolution; was in the battles of Bunker Hill, Long Island, White Plains, Trenton, Brandywine, Germantown, Saratoga, and Stillwater; was with the army in all their hardships at Valley Forge during the severe winter of '77–'78. He took an efficient part in Sullivan's expedition against the Six Nations, and was in chief command at Albany during the last summer of the war. Afterward he was appointed by his old commander and companion-in-arms, General Sullivan, then president of the state of New Hampshire, to command, as brigadier-general, all the forces of the state in a most critical juncture of the civil and military affairs of that section.

It is not so generally known that James Miller, who brought out more reputation from our last war with Great Britain at the northward than any other American save Winfield Scott, was a Scotch-Irishman out of the loins of Londonderry. He was born in Peterborough, N. H., in 1776; studied for a while in his youth at Williams College, in Massachusetts; became interested more or less in military affairs, and was recommended to the War Department at Washington by General Benjamin Pierce, father of the late President, and was commissioned major in the Fourth U. S. Infantry, March 3, 1809, the last day of Jefferson's administration. The war with England soon breaking out, young Miller was ordered to Indiana Territory under General Harrison, and his regiment was in the battle of Tippecanoe. Under General Hull at Detroit, James Miller and Lewis Cass, both young officers in the army, and the two becoming thereafter life-long friends, planted with their hands the United States flag on Canada soil, at Sandwich, July 14, 1812. Both were afterward taken prisoners with Hull, though Cass snapped his sword before surrendering it; and both made public complaint of what they deemed the cowardice of Hull, on the basis of which and other like testimony he was tried by court-martial and condemned, but was pardoned by the President, and lived to vindicate his action in a pamphlet now generally regarded as exculpatory and triumphant.

After Miller was exchanged he was put into command of the Twenty-seventh Regulars, and ordered to the Niagara frontier under General Jacob Brown. The story of the battle of Lundy's Lane is known to all Americans; but I have recently had the pleasure of reading a letter written by Colonel Miller three or four days after the battle to his wife — "My Beloved Ruth" — in which he gives interesting details of the storming of the battery and the capture of the cannon, which are not down in the books. Brown's order to him, as he transcribes it for his wife, is a little different from what it stands in the histories — "Colonel, take your regiment, storm that work, and take it!"   "I'll try, sir!"

With three hundred men he moved steadily up the hill in the darkness, along a fence lined with thick bushes, that hid his troops from the view of the gunners and their protectors, who lay near. When within short musket range of the battery, they could see the gunners, with their glowing linstocks ready to act at the word *Fire!* Selecting good marksmen, Miller directed each to rest his rifle on the fence, select a gunner, and fire at a given signal. Very soon every gunner fell, when the colonel and his men rushed forward and captured the battery — not, however, until a terrible hand-to-hand fight in the darkness with the protectors of the guns had ensued. The British fell back. Rallying, and being re-inforced by three hundred men sent forward by Drummond at Queenstown, they were repulsed the second time. Let Miller tell the rest of the story in words to his wife: "After Generals Brown, Scott, and others were wounded, we were ordered to return back to our camp, about three miles [Chippewa], and preparations had not been made for taking off the cannon, as it was impossible for me to defend them and make preparations for that too, and they were all left on the ground, except one beautiful six-pounder, which was presented to my regiment in testimony of their distinguished gallantry. The officers of this army all say, who saw it, that it was one of the most desperate and gallant acts ever known; the British officers whom we have prisoners say it was the most desperate thing they ever saw or heard of. General Brown told me the moment he saw me that I had immortalized myself. 'But,' said he, 'my dear fellow, my heart ached for you when I gave you that order, but I knew it was the only thing that would save us.'"

Miller had indeed immortalized himself already; and five years later, in the piping times of peace, he resigned his commission in the army, an act he regretted as long as he lived, and received the appointment of Governor of Arkansas, a place he held for four years. He returned to New Hampshire, an invalid, in 1823, and received the appointment of national collector at Salem and Beverly in Massachusetts, a post he held for twenty-four years, when he resigned, and was succeeded by his youngest son, who held it eight years longer. He was doubly immortalized in this last period of his life by having Nathaniel Hawthorne, a subordinate in the custom-house, "a chiel amang them taking notes"; and the notices of James Miller in the miscellaneous writings of Hawthorne honor the pen and heart of the one as much as the life and conduct of the other. Miller died 7th July, 1851, and lies buried in Salem. He was a Scotch-Irishman indeed, in whom was no guile.

Londonderry and the towns populated from it have furnished ornaments to society all over New England in every walk of life. Let me rather say, all over the country, particularly North and Middle and West. I will only mention two by name in this connection, Horace Greeley and George W. Nesmith. Greeley was a man known and read of all men. His faults were as open as his virtues, and both rested back alike upon a true and rough manhood.

> " Strong-armed as Thor — a shower of fire
>   His smitten anvil flung ;
>   God's curse, Earth's wrong, dumb Hunger's ire —
>   He gave them all a tongue ! "

George W. Nesmith died only a month ago, in his ninetieth year, and passed his life in the near neighborhood of Daniel Webster's birthplace in New Hampshire, both of them graduates of Dartmouth College, and the two remarkably intimate with each other till Webster's death in 1852, though Nesmith was by much the younger man. In the very crisis of the fate of his college, Webster defended and emancipated it in the Supreme Court of the United States; perhaps in part from that very reason, so strongly was the younger man drawn toward the traditions of the elder. Nesmith flung his old age, till the very last, into a supreme effort to sweeten and harmonize troubles that have come upon his college, not troubles of the same crucial type as struck it in the first quarter of the century, but still troubles that impede its usefulness and lessen its prestige.

I have no list of the governors of New Hampshire from 1775, when all direct authority of the British crown was suppressed there, and even if I had I could not certainly tell what proportion of them have been of Scotch-Irish origin; but I have been pretty familiar with the names of New Hampshire governors for fifty years, and I venture in this great presence the historical conjecture, that nearly, if not quite, one-half of them from that day to this have been of our own strain of blood.

3. KENNEBEC COUNTRY. Full as New Hampshire became of the Scotch-Irish, especially in the southern and eastern halves of it, it is likely that this element became still more predominant in what

is now the state of Maine. We have already noted the but half-suppressed anxiety of Governor Shute at Boston to get as many as possible of the five ship-loads into his province to the eastward, as a frontier-barrier against the French and Indians of Canada. Although many of the supposed three hundred persons who wintered in the harbor of Portland returned the next spring to the Merrimac to settle Londonderry, some of them remained in Maine. We know certainly, that John Armstrong, Robert Means, William Jameson, Joshua Gray, William Gyles, and a McDonald remained and founded families in Portland. James Armstrong, for example, an infant son of John, was born in Ireland in 1717, and the parents had a son Thomas, born in Portland in 1719. It is pretty certain, also, that parts of that company were left on points along Casco Bay and the mouth of the Kennebec, at or near Wiscasset, before the main part returned to the Merrimac.

We happen to know with almost absolute certainty the fortunes of one of the families left behind in Portland, when the future Londonderry settlers returned to Massachusetts. This was the family of Joshua Gray. He had a Celtic-Irish wife, and a large family. The names of the sons of this family were Reuben, Andrew, James, John, Samuel, and Joshua. In the spring of 1759, the year of Wolfe's battle on the Heights of Abraham, Governor Pownall, of Massachusetts, fitted out an expedition of three hundred and ninety-five men in order to capture from the French the mouth of the Penobscot River. They left Portland May 4, and arrived at Wasaumkeag Point, May 17. Among the enlisted men were Andrew and Reuben Gray. In Governor Pownall's journal may be found the following: "May 26. Visited Pentaget with Captain Cargill and twenty men. Found the old abandoned French Fort, and some abandoned settlements. Went ashore into the Fort. Hoisted the King's Colours there and drank the King's health. Embarked in the sloop King George for Boston."

The place thus described is now known as Castine, from Baron Castine, whose name is a very familiar one along the eastern coast of Maine; and among the twenty men who accompanied Governor Pownall on that occasion was Reuben Gray. A strong fort was planted at Wasaumkeag Point, and the work of building it was carried forward so diligently, that it was completed July 5, 1759, the expense being five thousand pounds. A garrison was kept there until 1775, when the fort was dismantled by Commodore Mowett in a British man-of-war, and later in the same year entirely destroyed by Colonel Cargill of New Castle. The building of this fort marked

the beginning of settlements by the English around the Penobscot
Bay and River region, the first settlers being members of the military
expedition, who, on being discharged, established themselves near
the fort, where their homes could have its protection against the
French and Indians. The two Gray brothers, Reuben and Andrew,
being of a venturesome disposition, crossed the bay and located at
what is now called Penobscot, and were the first settlers of English
origin to build their homes on that historic peninsula. Several
brothers of Reuben and Andrew followed them to the Penobscot,
and at last, also, their old father and mother. The distinction is
claimed for Reuben's son, Reuben Gray, 2d, of being the first male
child of English parentage born east of the Penobscot River, the
date of his birth being 1762. The old father, Joshua, died about
the opening of the Revolution, but the Irish widow continued until
after the close of the war. The first Reuben seems to have died
about 1820, and the second certainly in 1858; and about ten years
ago, as my two oldest boys, with other students of Williams College,
were making sailing excursions along the coast of Maine, they ran
across, at Brooksville, within the mouth of the Penobscot, Captain
Abner Gray, son of the second Reuben, then nearly eighty-five, as
straight as an arrow, helpful and hospitable; and that chance
acquaintance led to the correspondence that has given us these facts
about the Scotch-Irish on the Penobscot. The Grays of this very
family are still in large numbers in Brooksville and Bucksport, on
the lower Penobscot; and so are Wears, and Orrs, and Doaks, and
other Scotch-Irish families.

In published extracts from court records of the Province of
Maine I have read the affidavits of several of the early inhabitants,
who stated that they came to Boston in August, 1718, from Ulster,
and thence that autumn to Maine, where they settled in Brunswick and that neighborhood; which is another independent evidence that parts of our now famous five ship-loads furnished the
first Scotch-Irish settlers of Maine, as well as of New Hampshire
and Massachusetts.

The next attempt to introduce this class of immigrants into
Maine seems to have been from a source entirely independent of the
previous one, though nearly contemporaneous with it. Robert Temple, who had been an officer in the English army, and was a gentleman of family, was a leader in the enterprise. His motive was to
establish himself as a large landed proprietor in this country. He
says in a letter to the Plymouth proprietors: "In September, 1717,
I contracted with Captain James Luzmore, of Topsham, to bring

me, my servants, and what little effects I had to Boston." "My
eye," he continues, "was always toward a good tract of land as well
as a convenient place for navigation." Returning from an examina-
tion of Connecticut, he says: "I was resolved to see the eastern
country also before I should determine where to begin my settlement." The proprietors of the west banks of the Kennebec took
him down to see their land; but he gave the ultimate preference to
land on the east side of the river, which belonged to Colonel Hutch-
inson and the Plymouth Company, and he became a partner in that
concern and engaged to bring a colony to it. Within two years he
chartered five large ships to bring over families from Ulster to carry
on the settlement. They were the same sort of people that came to
Boston, and from the same general localities. During the two years,
1719 and 1720, several hundred families were landed on the shores
of the Kennebec from its mouth to Merrymeeting Bay. Many of
the families settled in what is now Topsham, which received its
name from Temple's place of departure on his first voyage, the port
of Exeter in Devonshire; another portion settled in the northerly
part of Bath, on a tract of land stretching along on Merrymeeting
Bay to the Androscoggin, and was called Cork, and sometimes Ireland, from the country of the settlers, which name it still retains;
and still others straggled along on the eastern side of the bay and
river, and descendants of these still occupy and improve portions of
the country. The familiar Scotch names, McFadden, McGowen,
McCoun, Vincent, Hamilton, Johnston, Malcolm, McClellan, Crawford, Graves, Ward, Given, Dunning, Simpson, still live to remind
the present generation of the land from which their ancestors came.

Unhappily, the Indian troubles, which we call "Lovell's War,"
commenced shortly after Temple's people got fairly seated on the
Kennebec, broke up some of the settlements, which had begun to
assume a flourishing aspect, and scattered away many colonists from
the rest; some of these sought a refuge with their countrymen at
Londonderry, N. H., but the greatest part of them removed to Penn-
sylvania; Brunswick and Georgetown were destroyed and deserted;
in the summer of 1722, nine families were captured at one time by
the Indians in Merrymeeting Bay; but Temple himself and many
of his people remained, and the descendants of both have connected
their names indissolubly with Bowdoin College in Brunswick, and
with both state and church in Maine. Temple himself received a
military commission from Governor Shute, and rendered good service
in the defense of his adopted country. His posterity have served it
long and well. His eldest son, Robert, married a daughter of Gov-

SCOTCH-IRISH IN NEW ENGLAND.

ernor Shirley; the second son, John, lived to become a baronet, and married a daughter of Governor Bowdoin, of Massachusetts. Their daughter, Elizabeth, married Thomas D. Winthrop, of Massachusetts, and those are the parents of Robert C. Winthrop, of Boston.

After the breaking up of the Norridgewock tribe on the Upper Kennebec, some of Temple's Scotch settlers returned to the deserted places on the eastern shore, and new adventurers sought the vacant seats. In 1729, Colonel Dunbar, a native of Ireland, of Scottish descent, in the hope of separating Maine from the Massachusetts government, obtained a commission from the crown as governor of the territory. He had previously been commissioned as surveyor-general of the woods, with a view to preserve the pine timber for the British navy. He selected Fort Frederick, at Pemaquid, as the seat of his government, and was placed in possession by a detachment of troops from Nova Scotia, in 1730. Rightful were the claims of Massachusetts to the eastern shore; but Dunbar took immediate measures to occupy and improve the lands in his new province by inviting his countrymen, the Scotch-Irish, to settle upon them through liberal inducements both of lands and privileges. He granted one-hundred-acre lots on Pemaquid in the neighborhood of the fort, laid out and improved a large farm for himself, and ceded to his countrymen, Montgomery and Campbell and McCobb, large tracts, which soon became towns. In the course of two or three years, more than one hundred and fifty families, principally of Scotch descent, were introduced into this territory. Some were drawn from the older settlements of the stock in Massachusetts and New Hampshire, and some were fresh colonists from Ireland. These had their pastor, Rev. Robert Rutherford, and their Presbyterian institutions, which they cherished with great tenacity for a long time. Among these families were McClintocks, Hustons, McLeans, McKeens, Caldwells, Dicks, Forbushes, Browns, McIntyres, and McFarlands.

Massachusetts continued to protest against the government of Dunbar, excellent as were its results, and it was terminated in August, 1732, and jurisdiction restored to Massachusetts. Dunbar returned to England in 1737, where, like Penn, he was committed to prison for debt, but afterward released through the liberality of his friends, and in 1743 was appointed governor of St. Helena, an English island since rendered famous by the exile of a more distinguished ruler than this early Scotch-Irish governor of Maine.

Samuel Waldo, who had been a sort of agent of Massachusetts in displacing Dunbar, and who had an interest in the territory as a patentee, and who had seen the benefit arising from the admirable class of immigrants whom Dunbar had introduced, proceeded to profit by the example in respect to his own ample possessions lying between the St. George and the Penobscot rivers. In 1734, Waldo carefully examined the resources of his land grant, and fortunately discovered the invaluable quarries of limestone, which have proven from that day to this day a source of continued riches and progress to the inhabitants of that peninsula. The first movements in the manufacture of lime there, which are now so extended, and which seem at present to claim the attention of our legislators at Washington, was so small that the lime was shipped to Boston in molasses casks. The St. George River, on which the first settlements were made, is a plunging stream, and afforded then and now fine mill sites for handling both wood and stone, and the near forests gave an abundant supply of timber.

Waldo's first settlers upon his eastern grant were all of Scotch descent from the North of Ireland — some of them of recent immigration, and others had been in the country from the first arrival in Boston in 1718. The company consisted of twenty-seven families, arrived upon the spot in 1735, and each family furnished with one hundred acres of land on the banks of the St. George, in the present town of Warren, Maine. The names of some of these pioneers will show to those familiar with the history of Maine how much the state is indebted to this enterprising proprietor, Samuel Waldo, for placing in permanent contact with the soil these most useful settlers. Among the names are Alexander, Blair, Kilpatrick, North, Patterson, Nelson, Starrett, Howard, McLean, Spear, Creighton, McCracken, and Morrison. The Old French War broke out in 1744, which greatly interrupted developments in Maine for ten years, when Waldo went to Scotland again, and formed a company of sixty adults and many children, who reached St. George's river in September, 1753, and were settled in the western part of Warren, to which they gave the name of Stirling, the ancient royal city of their country. These were mostly mechanics; the names of some of them were Anderson, Malcolm, Crawford, Miller, Auchmutey, Carswell, and Johnston; and this we believe to be the last immigration into New England of people of Scottish extraction, in any considerable number, prior to the outbreak of the Revolutionary War.

From these three centers of diffusion, now briefly indicated — Worcester, Londonderry, Wiscasset — the Scotch-Irish element penetrated and permeated all parts of New England: Maine the most of all, New Hampshire next, then Massachusetts, and then in lessening order Vermont and Connecticut and Rhode Island. They were all in general one sort of people. They belonged to one grade and sphere of life. They were for the most part very poor in this world's goods. The vast majority of all the adults, however, could read and write. If they had but one book to a family, that book was surely the Bible, which is itself, as we sometimes forget, a large collection of books of very varied character; and if there were two volumes to a family, the second place in most cases was disputed between Fox's "Book of Martyrs" and Bunyan's "Pilgrim's Progress." Their personal habits, their mental characteristics, their religious beliefs and experiences, and their very superstitions, were held largely in common; and all these were in more or less pronounced contrast with corresponding traits of the English Puritans who had nestled before them in most parts of New England.

So far as their physical natures went, they had received in the old country a splendid outfit for the race of life, in large bones and strong teeth, and a digestive apparatus the envy of the mountain bears. Men and women both were trained to an almost tireless physical industry. The struggle for physical subsistence had been with them no mere figure of speech. First of European countries, the potato had been found by Ireland, to which it had been brought from Virginia by slave-trader Hawkins in 1565, an invaluable resource of food for the poor; and each and every company of Scotch-Irish brought with them to New England, as a part of the indispensable outfit, some tubers of this esculent, which they prized beyond price. The pine lands of New England, which are always sandy, are adapted to the potato; and if there were no suffering from hunger in those large families during the first years of their sojourn, it should doubtless be put to the credit of the easily-cultivated, much-multiplying Irish potato!

Each and every company of these people brought also with them into New England the agricultural implements needful for the culture of the flax-plant, and the small wheels for spinning the flax-fiber, and the looms for weaving the linen textures. Nothing connected with the newcomers excited so much interest in English and Puritan Boston, in 1718, and the three following years, as the small wheels worked by women and propelled by the foot, for turning the straight flax-fibers into thread. There was a public exhibition of their skill in spinning flax, by the Scotch-Irish women, on Boston Common in the spring of 1719, at which prizes were awarded to the foremost. Drake's "Boston" gives an account of the sensation produced by the advent of this strange machine there, and of societies and schools formed to teach the art of thus making linen thread. For four years the novelty exercised its fascination, and the first ladies of the town paraded on the Common to exhibit their newly-learned art, derived from their stalwart sisters from over the sea. It is not historically set down in the records in so many words, but at this safe distance, and (as it were) under the protection of the guns of Fort Duquesne, we may venture the assertion, that the Boston girls were hard to beat in their newly-found and most useful avocation!

It is time now to conclude this paper, perhaps too long already, with some brief points of reference to common traits among them, to characteristics, some good, some bad, but very few indifferent! It is perfectly plain at every point of their settlement alongside the previous English Puritan, that they pretty soon excited prejudice against themselves, sometimes disgust, and sometimes even hate. The natural result of this was to throw them more and more upon each other in intermarriage, in a community of residence and of interest and of feeling; so that they did not coalesce very readily with other strains of blood and with other sects of Christians, so that they tended to keep up acquaintance in families from generation to generation, even when separated locally; and, consequently, the very traits themselves, the peculiarities, tended to preserve and perpetuate themselves for the ends of a later critical study and record.

a. In the first place, what is the contemporary testimony of the senses of those who came into personal contact with our Scotch-Irish ancestors who settled New England? The late Mr. Jewell, of Hartford, Conn., who was a tanner by trade, was sent by his country as a minister plenipotentiary to the court of St. Petersburg; being a Yankee, and "wanting to know you know," and being a tanner in possession of most of the profitable secrets of his guild, he went to Russia determined to avail himself of all his official and personal chances to find out the chemical composition and proportions of the tanning materials that give the peculiar odor and character to what is called "Russia leather"; but this was a national secret exceedingly profitable to the Muscovites; genial and precious as was dear Mr. Jewell, they would tell him nothing, but they would show him everything — were not Russia and the United States traditional and everlasting friends? Mr. Jewell told us himself on his return that he literally "followed his nose" in those Russian leather establishments; what he learned in this way he did not impart except to his partners, but he rightly considered the process to be one of inductive reasoning, the results of which were scientific and satisfactory to himself and his friends; in one word, that logical inferences may be drawn from the sense of smell as well as from the other senses, and that he was not shut up to "ocular demonstration," so far as the immemorial processes of tanning skins are concerned.

It is indisputable that the contemporaries of our Scotch-Irish ancestors in New England satisfied themselves by analogous trains of reasoning and conclusion that, in their new neighbors' scale of the virtues, personal cleanliness was put way down far below godliness! They began with a devout care of the spirit, and life was really not long enough for them to fetch round to a decent care of the flesh! Wash-bowl and pitcher was no part of the common setout of the newly-married pair. In the more progressive families an iron skillet in the kitchen sink opened up a chance for parents and children to wash their hands and faces in the morning, a chance, I take it, that rarely hardened itself into a rule for either. Ablution of the whole body even once a year, or ten years, or a life-time, was a thing practically unknown for three generations of our ancestral fathers and mothers. *Tertium quid?* This matter had ill consequences, of course, in diseases and mortality of children; in a disgust felt for uncleanly old people; in an intolerable stench arising from crowded religious assemblies, often prolonged for hours and hours; and in a prejudice and mockery on the part of neighbors trained in and accustomed to more cleanly personal habits.

For two or three generations, at least, ordinary houses were not provided with ordinaries of any kind; barns and pig-pens were in close proximity to the houses, and the two were scarcely discriminated from each other; the methods of farming were to the last degree uncleanly and unwholesome and disgusting—this is particularly noted in regard to Londonderry and its neighborhood, and I know that it was true in relation to Worcester. Their company was more or less avoided by the English on this account, and their rights doubtless less respected; the intermarriages that took place for two generations were for the most part with the lowest and poorest of the low and poor English; and with the major part of this class of people in New England the steps upward to the daily bath and the decent water-closet have been unreasonably slow and interrupted.

b. In the second place, it must be frankly admitted, that the dread of water in another sense of that term greatly harmed our folks for the first century of their residence in this land. They discriminated against water, in their estimate of beverages. Account for it as we may, high latitude, Celtic restlessness, strenuous poverty, aspiration above realization, cheap whisky, what not, the Scotch of

whatever origin and whatever residence grasp and hold too much
stimulus *per capita* of the population. It was always so. It is so
now. It is not because they are *canny*, and it is not because they
are Presbyterians. *I do not know the reason why.* If there be one
man in this vast assemblage that knows the reason and will tell it
straight, he will immortalize himself like James Miller, and this
four days' meeting in this year of grace will need no other memorial till the end of time !

When Londonderry was incorporated in the name of George III.,
June, 1722, the charter enacted "that on every Wednesday of the
week forever they may hold, keep, and enjoy a market for the buy-
ing and selling of goods, wares, and merchandise, and various kinds
of creatures, endowed with the usual privileges, profits, and immunities, as other market towns fully hold, possess, and enjoy ; and two
Fairs annually forever, the first to be held and kept within the said
town on the 8th day of November next, and so annually forever, and
the other on the 8th day of May in like manner. Provided, if it
should so happen, that at any time either of these days fall on the
Lord's day, then the said Fair shall be held and kept the day following it. The said Fair shall have, hold, and enjoy the liberties, privileges, and immunities as other Fairs in other towns fully possess,
hold, and enjoy."

For more than one hundred years these semi-annual fairs were
maintained without a break. Their original design was good ;
namely, to afford opportunity to people of neighboring towns to
meet and exchange their commodities with each other for a mutual
profit — and we will just note in passing that the Scotch-Irish of
that day had not made the grand modern discovery that exchange
of commodities is a crime to be prevented by the exercise of all the
powers of the United States government. The assemblages at these
fairs were usually large ; merchants from Haverhill and Salem and
Boston were present with their goods, and every variety of home
growths and manufactures was collected for exchange. Everything
at first was conducted with a decent order and propriety, although
the fair was always held in and around the only tavern of the town,
and there was always much drinking over the bar and some intoxi-
cation. As time went on and as stores became multiplied in the
towns, and as means of communication improved, the benefits of
these fairs and the grounds for their maintenance diminished, and
the obvious evils increased, until they proved a moral nuisance,
attracting chiefly the more corrupt portion of the community, and
exhibiting each year for successive days scenes of vice and folly in

some of their worst forms. Serious attempts were made from time
to time by the town to mitigate these evils, but with little success.
In 1798 the following vote was passed at the annual town-meeting:
" From the misconduct and disorderly behavior of most of the people
which frequent the fair, as now holden, the good intention and
original design are altogether defeated, it is hereupon enacted, that
it shall be confined to two days — one day each spring and fall;
voted also, that no booth shall be used after 9 o'clock in the evening
of said days, for selling merchandise or liquor, or furnishing any
kind of entertainment, without forfeiting and paying a fine of one
pound." And at last the final suppression of the fair was brought
about in 1839, as the result of the temperance reformation in Londonderry, for when the bar was removed from the tavern and no
intoxicating drinks were to be had in the place, the crowds assembled as usual, but at once withdrew.

Many of the social customs of our fathers indicate also a fond-
ness for strong drink, which not even their iron constitutions and
out-of-door life, and in the main, approving consciences, could prevent from demoralizing them. This love of liquor was a national
trait. The direct evidence we have on this point relates more
particularly to Londonderry and its resulting towns, but there are
lines of proof that converge upon the same point in relation to
Worcester and its sequels, and to the Kennebec and Penobscot towns
as well. It is true that, owing to the difference in their language
and habits and modes of life from those of their English neighbors,
prejudices against these settlers were early imbibed and unreasonably indulged, and many things in their manners and practices were
grossly exaggerated at the time and falsely reported and believed;
we must bear all this in mind in weighing the evidence, but the
traditions that have come down in certain families from generation
to generation, with some of which I became very familiar from
childhood to manhood, as well as the written record in all its varied
forms, can leave no doubt on the minds of their candid descendants
that here was a crevasse in the generally solid character of their
moral build-up. They found or made occasion in their marriage
ceremonies, in their wakes or watchings with the dead, and in their
funeral solemnities, to partake of ardent spirits with such freedom
and frequency as were often productive of most painful scenes and
serious consequences.

The wedding, for example, was in substance a sumptuous feast.
The invitations were given out at least three days before the time,
it being considered an affront to receive one only one day previous.

At the appointed hour the groom proceeded from his dwelling with his select friends, male and female; about half way on their journey to the house of the bride, they were met by the bride's select male friends; and, on meeting, each of the two companies made choice of one of their number "to run for the bottle" to the bride's house. The champion of the race who reached the well-filled bottle first, and returned with it, gave a toast, drank to the bridegroom's health, and having passed the bottle fully round, the united company proceeded to the residence of the bride. When arrived there, the religious and other services did not differ essentially from those common now at domestic weddings; but the ceremony being concluded, the whole company sat down to the entertainment, at which the "best man" and "best maid" presided. Then the room was cleared for dances and other amusements; the "flow" was kept up, and the "floor" was kept cleared; and an aged narrator, about the beginning of this century, kindling at the recollection of scenes then for him all gone by, concluded his account of the ancient wedding, "and the evening was spent with a degree of pleasure of which our modern fashionables are perfectly ignorant!"

When death entered a Scotch-Irish community in the olden time in New England, and one anywise prominent was removed, there was at once a cessation of all labor in the neighborhood. The people gathered at the house of mourning, and proceeded night after night to observe a custom which they had brought with them from Ireland (whether it be more Irish than Scottish, if there is any difference of meaning between these epithets in this connection, it were vain to speculate) called the "wake," or watching with the dead, until the interment had taken place. These night scenes, as at the present time wherever kept up, often exhibited a mixture of seriousness and frivolity, of religion and deviltry, to the last degree grotesque and incompatible. The Scriptures would be solemnly read, long prayers would be offered, and words of counsel and admonition administered to the mourning circle; but before long, according to established usage, the glass, with its exhilarating and intoxicating beverage, must circulate freely and repeatedly; so that, before the dawn, the joke and the laugh, if not scenes more boisterous and bewildering, would break in upon the slumbers of the dead.

The assemblage was sure to be large in all the Scotch-Irish settlements, whatever might have been the age or character or worldly condition of the party deceased, at the funeral services. Every relative, however distant the connection, must surely be present, or it would be regarded as a marked neglect; and it was expected also that all the friends and acquaintance of the deceased within a reasonable distance of the home would be in attendance. Funeral sermons were rarely or never delivered upon the occasion, yet there would usually be as large a congregation as assembled on the Sabbath. Previous to the prayer ardent spirit was always handed round, not only to the mourners and bearers, but also to the entire assembly. Again after prayer, and before the coffin was removed, the same thing was repeated. Nearly all would follow the body to the grave, and usually the greater number walked. Processions from a third to one-half a mile in length were not infrequent in Londonderry at the burial of an ordinary citizen. On their return to the house, the demoralizing draught was again administered to all, and a further edible entertainment provided. Many a poor family became embarrassed, if not absolutely impoverished, in consequence of the heavy expenses incurred, not so much by the sickness which preceded the death of one of its members, as by the funeral ceremonies as then and there observed, required, as they foolishly supposed, by respect for the dead.

c. In the third place, it was a pleasing and remarkable trait of these people, that they knew how to put things in a humorous and witty and even sarcastic dress. It was natural to them. They could do it well, and therefore they liked to do it. They were marvelously quick at repartee. Of course their brogue was a great help to them here, because it intensified the sense of incongruity, which seems to be of the essence of merriment. Subjectively they relished the sense of the grotesque and incongruous, and objectively their art and their brogue helped them to magnify it. Rev. Dr. Morrison once delivered an election sermon before the New Hampshire legislature, which proved incisive and effective; the body voted to print a specified number of copies, when a witty member (appreciating this point) moved to substitute an additional number, "provided they would also print the brogue."

The ministers were particularly skilled as between each other in humorous attack and retort. It was the one chief relief from the soberness and intensity of their lives. For example, two of these clergymen were walking along together on an icy road. Suddenly one of them slipped, and fell flat. Rev. Upright eyed his brother for a moment solemnly, and quoted: "The wicked stand in slippery places." Instantly retorted Rev. Prostrate, "I see they do, but I can't." William Stinson, born in Ireland, came to Londonderry with his father while still very young. Thence he migrated to Dunbarton, N. H., where he lived alone in his log-house, destitute of most of the conveniences of domestic life, and laid there and thus the foundations of a large fortune for the time. Rev. David McGregor, of Londonderry, called on him there (they had been boys together), and dined with him. Not having a table, or anything that would answer for a better substitute, Brother Stinson was obliged to make use of a bushel basket placed bottom-side upward. Both were grateful beforehand for the frugal meal frugally served, and Rev. Mr. McGregor, being asked, of course, to solicit the divine blessing, pertinently and devoutly implored that his host might be blessed "in his basket and his store." This was literally verified in the time to come!

Rev. Matthew Clark, who carried to his grave an unhealed wound from a sword-cut received in the siege of Derry, was accustomed, even to old age, and even in the pulpit, to quick and witty turns, which we must suppose were very effective. At any rate, they are very interesting to us, accustomed as we are, more or less, to dull preaching. The old cavalry captain with the black patch over his eye-brow was preaching one day on the over-confidence of Peter, that he would never deny his Lord, and his subsequent humiliating fall, and remarked: "Just like Peter, aye mair forrit than wise, ganging swaggering about wi' a sword at his side; an' a puir han' he mad' o' it when he cam' to the trial, for he only cut off a chiel's lug, an' he ought to ha' split down his head!"

This same old warrior of God is said also to have commenced a discourse from Philippians 4, 13, in the following startling manner: "'I can do all things.' Ay, can ye, Paul? I'll bet ye a dollar o' that (placing a Spanish milled dollar upon the desk). Stop! let's see what else Paul says: 'I can do all things through Christ, which strengthened me.' Ay, sae can I, Paul; I draw my bet," and he thereupon returned the dollar to his pocket!

This gift of enlivening humor, so common and so much cultivated among them, afforded a much-needed relief to their isolated lives upon their slovenly-kept farms, and afforded a relief also to their usually downright and dogmatic expression of their opinions. They were open and above-board in all their opinions and in all their talk. They did not back-bite with their tongues. There was biting, a plenty of it, but it was in a forward movement, fronting the opponent, whoever he was. Subterraneanism was something these people abhorred. If any one had a ground of complaint against another, or, what was much the same thing, if he supposed he had, his method of procedure was not like that of besieging castles in the Middle Ages, by gradual approaches, but, on the contrary, was exceedingly

direct and personal. The party of the second part was pretty sure
to be the first one to hear of the grievance, and of the quick feelings
excited by it. They seemed to like to fight their own battles directly,
and rarely enlisted substitutes! They were a pugnacious people
among themselves, these Scotch-Irish. Their views were mostly
definite, and sharpened to a point. There was a wholesome breezi-
ness among them that is refreshing to look back upon. They were
fond of regarding the Christian course under St. Paul's favorite
figure of a warfare; whatever else they failed to do, they meant to
fight a good fight, and to keep the faith once delivered to them —
the present saints. But in all this their ever-present sense of humor,
and their ability to bring it to bear in extremities, was not only a
relief to their pig-headed dogmatism, but was also a constant restraint
and antidote to it.

And yet, what seems at first blush to be incompatible with what
has just been said, it was a very common trait of these peculiar
people to maintain a sort of secrecy or clandestinism in matters
neutral to religion and politics, in matters personal and indifferent,
that stood in strange contrast to their utter frankness and unreserve
in those things which they deemed cardinal. They seem to have
caught beforehand, and to have practiced from generation to generation, the spirit of Burns's strain:

> "Conceal yersel' as weel's you can
> Frac critical dissection;
> But keek through every ither man
> Wi' sharpened sly inspection!

> "Ay free, aff han' your story tell,
> When wi' a bosom crony;
> But still keep something to yersel'
> Ye'll scarcely say to ony!"

Somewhere in the neighborhood of these two traits, which seem
themselves to be the opposites of each other, there lay another characteristic of this tribe, what might almost be called in Bacon's phrase
an idol of the tribe, — a persistent capacity to hold a grudge! I will
not philosophize upon this, though I am certain of it as a fact. To
forgive and forget an injury, real or supposed, a grace hard enough
of attainment for any Christian anywhere, God knows, and we know,
was especially hard for these half-Celtic and half-Saxon believers in
and imitators of the blessed Lord. We need to make no reference
here to the old historic feuds, Highland or Lowland — we are not
sure as that would have any relevancy; but any analysis of the

character of the New England Scotch-Irish, however cursory, in contrast with the English Puritans alongside of whom they lived and labored, would be faulty and out of the true, that did not call a passing attention to a characteristic of them, both men and women — a characteristic which has come down within the observation of those still living — a tendency to hold together and re-knit at intervals the strong fibers of a grudge, a prejudice, a misconception; fibers late and last to be fused in the blessed fires of Christian discipline and holy love!

d. And this brings us, in the fourth place, to some peculiarities in the religious conceptions and experience of these good people which may prove instructive and illuminating to us to whom these ends of the world have come. John Knox had adjusted for their simple eye-sight all the glasses in the long tube, pointed for them toward Geneva and John Calvin, whenever they wished to take their bearings from the east, and to renew the grounds and the proportions of the famous Five Points; and, at one and the same time, perform the impossible task so often undertaken to no purpose, to conform their lives in simple faith and love to the still, small voice, and to settle themselves theologically four-square and impregnable. Of course there was something grotesque in this attempted combination, and of course there was something sublime in it. John Calvin was only twenty-six years old when he wrote or sketched his famous "Institutes of Theology." Oh! that he had waited twenty-five years longer, and learned, as he certainly would have done, that men are made in the image of God in other respects also, as well as in a tendency to an inflexible logic-handling of data imperfectly understood! This would have saved our morbidly conscientious ancestors from much that appears to us insane and ridiculous; and, let it be confessed, would have prevented them also from undertaking much that proved great and enduring.

The Scotch-Irish Presbyterians of New England were in bondage to the "letter," and the "Emancipation Proclamation" has not even yet been read and pondered and joyfully accepted by many of their descendants. Contrary to the doctrine of St. Paul, who was and is the evangelist of the whole circle, they "served in the oldness of the letter and not in the newness of the spirit." They did not find out what this meaneth even from the lips of their own preferred teacher — "the letter killeth but the spirit giveth life." There was accordingly, a hardness and a formality in their religious lives and actions, in striking contrast with the relative freedom and love and spirit of the best Christians of our own times, who may themselves have come out from the rigid lines and mailed loins of these saints and soldiers of the Middle Age.

The cases of church discipline, many of which have come down to us by way of record, turned for the most part not on the absence of brotherly love and the spirit of mutual helpfulness, which are of the essence of Christianity, but on some miserable technicality, some formal violation of an external rite or usage of the church. For example, the Thursday before communion was a fast day, and kept with all the rigidity and punctilio of a Jewish Sabbath. A complaint was brought against a member of the church of Londonderry, for spreading out grain to dry on such a Thursday — the grain was ready to spoil for lack of the sun shining in his strength — and he was duly and solemnly admonished by the session. In 1734, we find a complaint against John Morrison, brought by Archibald Stark, that the former, having found an axe in the road, "did not leave it at the next tavern as the laws of the country doth require"; and though Morrison acknowledged the fact, and plead that the axe was of so small value that it would not quit the costs of legally proclaiming it, yet he was severely censured by the session, "and exhorted to repent of the evil."

The cheap metallic pieces, called "tokens," which entitled the bearer without question to the privileges of the Lord's Supper, came to have a factitious and even superstitious value set upon them by the holders, as if St. Peter himself, at the gate of heaven, must instantly recognize the validity of those dirty bits of brass stamped with the initials of the church. Amid so much that was outer and formal and Jewish and rectangular, there is of necessity lacking the sweeter and gentler virtues, the noiseless charity, the reaching out to one another the hands which are felt, not seen. All the rain from heaven seemed to come in great showers in the day-time, and there was less of the refreshing and universal dew, the gift of the night, found often on the under-side of the blade and the leaf and the flower.

The bolder and sterner virtues of the Christian character were those present — the vigilance of the watchman on the walls of Zion, the valor of the desperate onset summoned by the trumpet of Jehovah, the tirelessness of the strong reaper in the hot harvest-field, the dying cry of the born general, sleepless and intent, "Tête d'armée!" But alas! for the onesidedness of the best human life; alas! for the temptation that lurks the nearest to the noblest virtue; alas! for the exhibition of what is devilish in apparently vital connection with what is divine. So here. Our fathers were heresy-hunters.

They revered a shibboleth. They only could guard aright the ark of God. They thought themselves to be vicegerents. They fell into the sin of condemning their brethren, for whom Christ died.

> "The Truth's worst foe is he who claims
>   To act as God's avenger;
> And dreams beyond his sentry beat
>   The crystal walls in danger!

> "Who sets for heresy his traps
>   Of verbal quirk and quibble;
> And weeds the Garden of the Lord
>   With Satan's borrowed dibble."

I may be wrong in this, but it is my deliberate judgment, that the English Pilgrims of the Old Colony and their descendants, and the original Puritans of the Massachusetts Bay and their children, fallible and narrow and one-sided and bigoted and uncharitable as they all were, nevertheless represented on the whole, in an age equally adverse to them all, a sweeter and better and truer spirit in their lives than the more highly organized and more historically connected Christians whose blessed memories we strive to keep alive to-day.

However this may be, one thing is certain, New England has proved to the last degree inhospitable to Presbyterianism as a form of church administration. Established over and over again in Maine, in New Hampshire, and in fewer numbers in Massachusetts, renewed over and over again when decayed and moribund, the presbyteries have run one steady and inevitable course toward extinction. There is one nominal presbytery in New England to-day doing duty only on the official records of the church, denominated "Boston," but it was utterly unrepresented in the General Assembly last week at Saratoga. It has a name to live, but it is dead.

Something corresponding with what the evolutionists style "environment" must be the explanation of this most striking and reiterated phenomenon. What is there in New England that is so fatal to the Presbyterian form? A good word is oftentimes a harbor of refuge to the perplexed and baffled inquirer. Presbyterianism came to us early; it came strong; it reinforced itself from time to time with new and large recruits, but it could not root in Yankee land. What has been the matter? I answer, environment, whatever that may mean. The Plymouth people, from 1620 and onward, were obliged to take to independence in church government, whether they willed or nilled; ten years later and onward, John Winthrop and

his learned ministers in Charlestown, Cambridge, and Boston, drank
in from the salt marshes and Massachusetts Bay long whiffs of what
afterward came to be called Congregationalism; Roger Williams
inhaled the same sort of air in Salem, and liked the oxygen of it,
and carried it in stout lungs to Providence, to become the breath of
life to the Baptists, a vast congeries of independent churches; the
molds got set in New England; self-governed churches took the bits
in their teeth one by one; and when, in 1718, the Presbyterians
came to Boston, and triangulated themselves at Worcester, Londonderry, and Wiscasset, they established their own forms at the two
latter places without let or hindrance, but the opposition at Worcester was significant; and the whole trend and drift of things — in
short, the environment — was and has continued such, that, proud
of their fathers of every name, and thankfully accepting the tribute
from every land, New England people believe in and will uphold the
independent government of their churches, each for and by itself.

e. In the last place, we must note the social and political tenden-
cies and peculiarities of the Scotch-Irish in New England. It is
here that the main lesson comes in. It is here that their impress
has been deepest and best. It is along this line that we can clearly
trace their footsteps from the first, and see their lasting influence to
this day. There is no careful investigation but brings its surprises.
There is no genuine study of aggregate men whose results do not
display apparent contradictions at some point. It is so with our
folks. They were zealous Presbyterians, and that system implies
authority and subordination; the simple church member is under
the direction of the session to an extent unknown in independent
churches; the session is a part of the presbytery, and is controlled
by it; and all the presbyteries are under the legislative domination
of the general assembly. The system involves, therefore, higher
and lower in church authority; it involves rank in a certain sense,
and it would not seem to be favorable to individualism in rights and
power. Each intermediate grade, like the centurion in the Gospel,
says: "I also am a man under authority, having soldiers under me."

We should expect beforehand, accordingly, that these people
would be no great sticklers for individual rights in politics, and no
very sharp opponents of that insidious privilege, which is all the
while stealing a march on the rights of the masses, and creating by
law or usage privileged classes, lower and higher, polite plunderers,
and perhaps unconscious plundered. Sir Thomas More wrote of the
England of his time, and it is just as true of the United States in
each and every decade of the first century of the constitution: "The

rich are ever striving to pare away something further from the daily
wages of the poor by private fraud, and even by public law, so that
the wrong already existing, for it is a wrong that those from whom
the state derives most benefit should receive the least reward, is
made yet greater by means of the law of the state. The rich devise
every means by which they may in the first place secure to themselves what they have amassed by wrong, and then take to their
own use and profit, at the lowest possible price, the work and labor
of the poor. And so soon as the rich decide on adopting these
devices in the name of the public, then they become law."

On the contrary, rather in contrast with the Puritans, who, speak-
ing generally, seem to have felt no repugnance to distinctions and
privileges for themselves and their own, either in church or state,
these Scotch-Irish citizens, as a rule, manifested a working instinct,
if not a trained principle, favorable to equality of opportunity for
all men under the law, and hostile to special privileges to any, and
especially privileges to some at the expense of the rest. As the two
great simple elements of our domestic national politics were slowly
formulating themselves under the administration of Washington —
the two simple elements which have dominated our national politics
ever since, and served as the one stable foundation of our two political parties — our tribe in New England sided with Jefferson in his
pronounced views of state rights in opposition to centralization, and
of equality in opposition to privilege. Jefferson's religious views,
as they were represented in New England, were enormously unpop-
ular among all classes; but the instinct, if not the intelligence, of
the Scotch-Irish, led them to general approval of his political propo-
sitions; and as time went on and the results were brought into relief,
they ranged themselves generally under the Democratic banners,
particularly in New Hampshire and that part of Massachusetts
which is now Maine.

Hamilton's opposite construction of equality of rights, and of
national powers as over against the states, found greatly more favor
among the Puritan merchants of the bay, and among the Congregational clergy generally, than among the farmers and citizens of
Presbyterian antecedents. The father of the late "Long Jim"
Wilson, of Peterborough, N. H., was a Federalist, and his more distinguished son was a Whig, which means the same thing; and if *his*
son, the brave General Wilson of our late civil war be a Republican,
as I infer from heredity only, that means the same thing too. The
Wilson family in successive generations has been distinguished on
many grounds and in many members, but the mere fact, that the

Federalism of the ancestor is noted in Scotch-Irish records, emphasizes the other fact, that the greater part of his compeers took the other view. When I was a boy in New Hampshire, I used to hear "Long Jim" harangue Whig audiences on the efficacy of Whig doctrines with apparently tremendous effect; but when the election day came round, even in the universal fervor of 1840, the rank and file of Democratic yeomen rallied unbroken majorities against privilege and centralization. The "Granite State" is not more granite in its rocks than it has been, and will be, in its opposition to all schemes of whatever color, designed to rob the masses of men for the special benefit of a privileged few, and those designed also to make top-heavy and unwieldy the central structure of our complicated government, at the expense of the older and safer and more responsive, because more local, seats of political power.

Samuel Taggart also, born in Londonderry in 1754, minister in Colerain, Mass., for forty-one years, 1777–1818, a graduate of Dartmouth College in 1774, a man of gigantic stature, a member of Congress from a district of Western Massachusetts for seven successive terms, 1803–17, was nominally a Federalist, yet in reality and at bottom, like most of the rank and file of his people in Massachusetts, no friend of privilege and centralization. Indeed, he was a typical Scotch-Irishman. He was a politician and a preacher at the same time and among the same people. No incongruity suggested itself as between these functions to him or to them. They steadily supported him in both relations, and he faithfully represented them in both. "Where did you leave those few sheep in the wilderness?" inquired sarcastically John Randolph of Roanoke, of Taggart on the floor of the House. He had not left them. He thoroughly studied his colleagues at Washington in both branches; read his Bible through every winter he was there; possessed the confidence of Jefferson and Madison, fellow Scotch-Irish from Virginia, during both the entire presidential terms of both, though he did not go to Washington quite early enough to welcome there, and probably would not have heartily welcomed there, Rev. John Leland, his Baptist brother, when he took on the mammoth cheese as a testimonial to Jefferson of the political confidence of the people of Cheshire, in my own county of Berkshire. Taggart wrote and published, on the "Evidences of Christianity," on "British Impressments from our Marine," on the "Final Perseverance of the Saints," and many sermons and orations and addresses.

Political instinct in distinction from political intelligence in the masses of our countrymen, and particularly in the masses of our immigrants, as leading them to unite with one or other of the two great parties, each holding with remarkable continuity on the whole the tradition of its origin and the lines of its demarcation, has not yet received the attention and the respect from our public men which are its due. Men are not machines. There is a reason in their movements as well in their aggregate as in their individual capacity. And when the curse of money is removed from its corrupting place at or near our ballot boxes, as it will be, it will then be seen, that men native and naturalized choose their party from impulses and impressions only partly explicable even to themselves; and that there are drifts and currents God-impelled, as well as those distinctly started in the human reason, all which are sweeping on toward

> "That fair future day,
> Which fate shall brightly gild."

In conclusion, let me mention just a few living Scotch-Irish people out of the New England stock, with whom I chance to be acquainted directly or indirectly, whose acquaintance I highly prize, and who are each and all distinguished in their sphere: Hugh McCulloch, born and bred in Maine, known and honored of all men; Charles J. McCurdy, a nonagenarian jurist of Lyme, Conn.; Manton Marble, of New York; George W. Anderson, of Boston; Rev. Dr. George Mooar, of Oakland, Cal.; Miss Philena McKeen, Andover, Mass.; Mrs. Gov. Fairbanks, St. Johnsbury, Vt.; Robert C. Mack, Londonderry, N. H.; Senator Blair, and Congressman Moore, and Acting Governor Taggart, all of New Hampshire; Professor L. W. Spring, of Williams College; Major H. B. McClellan, of Kentucky, and Henry H. Anderson, of New York.

PARTIAL LIST OF AUTHORITIES.

1. Lincoln's History of Worcester.

2. Wall's Reminiscences of Worcester.

3. Worcester Records of Births and Deaths.

4. Registry of Deeds, Worcester.

5. Published Inscriptions on Gravestones in Worcester.

6. Parker's Londonderry, N. H.

7. State Papers of New Hampshire, particularly "Towns," vol. 14, and "Muster-Rolls," vol. 2.

8. Communications from Robert C. Mack, Londonderry, N. H.

9. Holland's History of Western Massachusetts, "Colerain," "Blandford," "Pelham," and *passim*.

10. History of Peterborough, N. H.

11. McKeen's History of Bradford, Vt.

12. Thompson's Gazetteer of Vermont, "Londonderry," "Landgrove," etc.

13. Caleb Stark's Life of John Stark.

14. American Biography, *sub verbis*, "Matthew Thornton," "Asa Gray," "Charles J. McCurdy," etc., etc., etc.

15. Hugh McCulloch's "Memorials of Half a Century."

16. Green's "Short History of England," as revised by Mrs. Green.

www.ingramcontent.com/pod-product-compliance
Lightning Source LLC
Chambersburg PA
CBHW030721110426
42739CB00030B/1130